SURELY IT CAN'T JUST BE ME . . .

Surely It Can't Just Be Me...

UNPUBLISHED LETTERS
TO
The Daily Telegraph

EDITED BY KATE MOORE

Quarto

First published in 2024 by Aurum Press,
an imprint of The Quarto Group
One Triptych Place, 185 Park Street,
London, SE1 9SH, United Kingdom

www.quarto.com/aurum

A catalogue record for this book is available from the British Library.

ISBN: 978-0-7112-9541-4
Ebook: 978-0-7112-9542-1

10 9 8 7 6 5 4 3 2 1

Typeset in Mrs Eaves by SX Composing DTP, Rayleigh, Essex

Printed and bound by CPI Group (UK) Ltd, Croydon, CR0 4YY

CONTENTS

INTRODUCTION

Momentous events often have us looking back as well as forward. On 5 July this year, we all woke up to a radically altered political landscape. After one of the most bizarre election campaigns in memory – one in which Rishi Sunak struggled to claw his way back from the moment of his rain-sodden announcement – Labour took control with a thumping majority. And so this, the 16th edition of the *Unpublished Letters* series, enters a new age. And readers are entitled to ask, not just "what's next?", but also "What *happened*?"

The answer is: really quite a lot. Since *Am I Alone in Thinking...?* was published in 2009 we have seen seven prime ministers, five general elections and one Larry the Downing Street cat. David Cameron rose, resigned and resurfaced as Lord Cameron; talk of "strong and stable government" under Theresa May evaporated under Boris "shopping trolley" Johnson. Poor Liz Truss lasted just long enough to see in the Carolean Age, before Rishi Sunak bounded in with promises to make the "difficult decisions" ducked by his predecessors. Alongside this never-ending political soap opera, we've weathered Brexit, a pandemic and a cost-of-living-crisis; cheered Team GB on at four Summer Olympics, and gritted our teeth through 15 iterations of the Eurovision Song Contest.

These and other momentous events are reflected in the emails (and still the occasional handwritten letter) that find their way to us every day. Browsing through the inbox, I am heartened to see how the good spirits of the *Telegraph*'s readers have prevailed through the most interesting of times. This year they have remained admirably sanguine in the face of the Conservatives' historic defeat. One noted cheerfully that this marked the 17th time he had backed a losing candidate; another expressed disappointment that Sir Ed Davey had not continued his pre-election antics and celebrated by jumping into the Thames. With Labour ensconced, readers lost no time in poring over the new Government's green energy policy and the revived plans to stub out smoking. Looking across the Atlantic, they watched, sometimes through their fingers, as the race for the White House swung between farce and high-stakes drama.

Almost as agonising for spectators was the wait to see how England would fare in the Euros. Was it an ill omen, one wonders, that Saint Jude (Bellingham) is the patron saint of lost causes? Why can't drawn games be decided by the total number of tattoos belonging to each team? And can we blame climate change for the final result? For those uninterested in sport, there has been plenty of excitement elsewhere, whether from *The Great British Sewing Bee* or the BBC's apocalyptic weather forecasts. Others got their thrills from navigating the potholes outside their driveway, or by making a drinking game out of the utterances of politicians. Our readers certainly know how to have fun.

Over the years the Letters Desk has seen some changes. There are fewer missives about *Downton Abbey*, MPs' duck houses, or Boaty McBoatface. Since Nicola Sturgeon quit the scene, the supply of fish jokes to our inbox has dried up. Yet much remains constant. Public figures still find themselves mired in sex scandals – though it is just as likely, these days, to be a *sext* scandal. We're still taking newsreaders to task over their pronunciation and struggling to spot the April Fool's Day joke in a world of preposterous headlines.

Our letter writers are bold with their opinions. Always open to new experiences, they continue to embrace the latest technologies (one writes of his extramarital affair with his "robomop"), and to stay abreast of evolving language trends ("For how much longer," wonders another, "must we see the microblogging site referred to as 'X, formerly Twitter'?"). Add to this their musings on the whims of fashion and dietary fads; the perils of getting older, getting fitter, or getting drunk; and the difficulty of maintaining a smoking habit as a volunteer fireman, and you have, I hope, a rounded portrait of modern life in all its absurdity.

As ever, my thanks must go to the team at Quarto; to Patricia Wynn Davies for casting a legal eye over everything; to Matt for the splendid cover cartoon, and to the Letters Desk editor Orlando Bird, who has kept us chugging along admirably over the last year. Finally, I must thank the readers themselves, for their inexhaustible supply of wit and wisdom. If ever you feel like it might just be you against the world, dip into this collection, and spend some time in their company.

Kate Moore
London SW1

FAMILY TRIALS AND TRIBULATIONS

Unexpected item in the bagging area

SIR – There is a saying that the difference between men and women lies in the handling of shopping lists. Men reputedly buy exactly what is on the list, no more, no less. Against this though, I must offer the experience of a friend of mine who was sent out by his wife to the local Aldi supermarket with a list of various household foodstuffs. He came back with a two-person tent. Nothing else.

Will Price
Port Erin, Isle of Man

SIR – Yesterday my friend went to the local shop for a loaf of bread. His wife shouted after him: "Can you get me some mints, please?"

He returned with 1lb of best lean beef mince.

Wendy May
Hereford

SIR – I once asked my husband to go and buy me a lemon. He returned with a melon.

I asked him to return it and bring home a lemon, and he went back and returned with a grapefruit. He refused to go back, so I ended up having to go and purchase the lemon myself.

Felicity Guille
London SW6

SIR – I send my husband shopping with two lists, one of things we need, and one of things we don't need. He loves a bargain!

Liz Appleby
Alnwick, Northumberland

SIR – When we reached the supermarket checkout my four-year-old son asked in his most helpful and loud voice if I had the cat food for our sandwiches.

I decided there and then not to give the cat any more of our tinned tuna.

Alex Scott
Tredington, Warwickshire

SIR – My husband recently went onto a well-known website to purchase suppositories. He was relieved to read that the ones for sale were classed as "new". A description of "used" would be unthinkable.

Anon
Via email
(You will understand why I don't wish my husband to be identified.)

SIR – Now that John Lewis has started selling sex toys, perhaps it should consider playing some background music in its stores. Could I suggest the Beach Boys' *Good Vibrations*?

Helen Hopwood
Cromer, NSW, Australia

SIR – John Lewis is my comfort zone.

Pauline Heigham
Nayland, Suffolk

SIR – Jane Shilling is wrong to suggest that lockdown destroyed our ability to speak to one another. I found myself thanking the self-service checkout machine yesterday, if that counts.

Mark Solon
London E1

SIR – After struggling to cope with the self-service checkouts that Waitrose chose to force upon us, one needs five minutes in the car to take in the free coffee and attempt to regain a sense of normality.

Michael Draper
Nether Wallop, Hampshire

Delivery targets

SIR – Reports that Amazon will be launching drone deliveries in 2024 will be welcomed by clay pigeon shooting enthusiasts.

Sandy Pratt
Storrington, West Sussex

SIR – Today I saw, with my own eyes, a clean Deliveroo bag. I had to tell someone.

Dr Edgar de Blieck
Via email

SIR – WHS is the brand name of British archaeologists' preferred trowel. I hope the news agents' re-branding advisers have prepared their hapless client for an increase in scruffy, very muddy and frustrated "diggers".

Michael Heaton
Warminster, Wiltshire

SIR – I didn't think the British economy was so bad until I noticed Poundland was employing security guards in-store.

Tony Cowan
Elgin, Moray

All comes out in the wash

SIR – When I became an RAF apprentice I was put in the gentle care of Corporal "Plod" Evans. His Health and Safety brief still comes to mind whenever I encounter an iron: "Right boys, the important thing is the 'ot bit goes down."

Squadron Leader T J W Leyland RAF (retd)
Boston, Lincolnshire

SIR – In the early days of our marriage over 40 years ago my wife ironed my shirts. One day I noticed while at work that one side of the shirt front I was wearing hadn't been ironed. I stupidly mentioned it to my wife. I've ironed my own shirts ever since.

Stephen Gledhill
Evesham, Worcestershire

SIR – Just before my first marriage broke up my wife taught me to iron my own shirts; something good came from it.

Rob Dorrell
Bath, Somerset

SIR – Back in the 1970s very large collars were in fashion.
My friend Brian's wife told him that she could only manage to iron one side of the collar in the morning and would have to iron the other side after lunch.

Francis Bongiovanni
Cheltenham, Gloucestershire

SIR – The only time my ironing basket was empty was during Wimbledon.

Trish Galli
Shaldon, Devon

Handy men

SIR – Am I the only husband that is totally useless with clingfilm? Every wrapping takes a minimum of two attempts because I consistently parcel one of my hands. With the amount that I get through, I should buy shares in the company.

Dave Alsop
Gloucester

SIR – I have noticed recently that some loo rolls unravel spontaneously into a bedraggled heap on the floor. Is this due to a change in the tensile strength of each sheet, in which case there are serious implications for the user, or poor-quality control in the rolling process?

It needs to be fixed, preferably before the general election.

Malcolm Allen
Berkhamsted, Hertfordshire

SIR – Has anyone else noticed that these new-fangled twist caps on bottles of tonic water/soda etc are almost impossible to open unless you are fortunate enough to own a chainsaw?

Ian Cribb
Poole, Dorset

Dressed to impress

SIR – Having worn white buttoned-down shirts for several decades as standard everyday dress, and now knowing that Prince George favours them too, I was most disappointed to be omitted from your Best Dressed List.

Nick Stewart
London SW6

SIR – At the Masters golf in Augusta, Sergio Garcia has been slated by the media for his yellow trousers and green shirt, which has been likened to a kitchen sponge.

Golfers for some inexplicable reason have always dressed, how shall we say, extravagantly and in times past the American John Daly dressed in colours that even Jackson Pollock probably never thought of.

In my youth I attended a garden party dressed the exact opposite of Garcia: bright green trousers and a yellow shirt. I was extremely hurt when a friend said I looked like a f-----g daffodil. We haven't spoken for a while.

Martin Henry
Good Easter, Essex

SIR – Your article lists "The dos and don'ts of wearing trainers with suits". May I offer some sound sartorial advice: don't.

Carl Brumpton
Ticehurst, East Sussex

SIR – Billy Joel amassed a multimillion-pound fortune and achieved induction into the coveted Rock and Roll Hall of Fame by wearing trainers with a suit. I'll try it.

Joe Swinnerton
Altrincham, Cheshire

SIR – I understand that the see-through shoe is this season's decisive, if divisive, footwear trend.

I've had one or two pairs over the last few decades, not realising I was a fashion leader – they're called sandals.

Fred Fearn
Bridport, Dorset

SIR – Why do car salesmen invariably wear pointy shoes? I'm waiting for my car to be serviced and it's like watching the film *Elf*.

Jo-Ann Rogers
Stoke-on-Trent, Staffordshire

SIR – I see that Ascot's creative director has backed neckties with dresses in an attempt to inspire fashionable female racegoers.

During the 1960s as a young teenager I sported a short dress with a necktie. Unfortunately the dress was lime green and adorned with a multicoloured "kipper" tie.

Lynette Chandler
Abergavenny, Monmouthshire

SIR – I am wearing a 72-hour heart monitor. I now know why Marks and Spencer pyjama bottoms have pockets.

Peter Watson
Sherborne, Dorset

SIR – The recent correspondence on pyjamas has been interesting and enlightening and one can only hope that an enterprising tailoring outfit on Savile Row will now design a smart three-piece set for the gentleman who takes working from home seriously.

Ken Nicholson
Glasgow

Wise head, young shoulders

SIR – Last week my 10-year-old grandson pointed at my flat cap and told me it was "iconic". I now look at it in a completely new light.

Robert Deighton
London SW6

SIR – It is a well-known fact that wearing a baseball cap automatically reduces one's intelligence by 10 per cent. Wearing it back-to-front reduces it by 50 per cent.

John Hamperl
Oxhey, Hertfordshire

SIR – The only acceptable day-to-day form of male headwear is a flat cap.

However, it should never be worn indoors, other than in the tap room or public bar of your local pub.

In very hot weather I suppose a baseball cap is just about permissible, just as long as you are away from home so no one will recognise you.

Jonathan L Kelly
Yatton, North Somerset

Take it on the chin

SIR – My recipe for a happy marriage lasting 60 years? Shave last thing at night, chaps; a lady does not appreciate getting into bed with someone whose face resembles a hedgehog.

Dick Kirby
Great Whelnetham, Suffolk

SIR – My beard appeared when my new wife and I went camping in Scotland in 1976.

I forgot to take my razor. She said it was like going round with a tramp, but it was reasonably established by the time we got home. It has stayed with me for 48 years and my children and grandchildren have known me no other way, so it will probably see me out.

David Dunbar
Broadway, Gloucestershire

SIR – Shortly after my wife and I were married, in 1967, she stated that, should I ever shave off my beard, she would leave me. I am very happy to report that we have just celebrated our 56th wedding anniversary.

Howard Farthing
Enfield, Middlesex

SIR – Having sported a beard for over 50 years I can assure you that in most cases it is the one thing that a man can do better than his wife.

Mick Clews
Daventry, Northamptonshire

SIR – My brother who ran a chain of estate agency offices once advertised: "Branch Manager required. No beards." I assume that this was directed to both sexes, so no discrimination there.

Luke Grant
Pensax Common, Worcestershire

Body images

SIR – Julius Caesar was allegedly impressed by his first sighting of British natives as their bodies were painted with woad, a bluish dye.

Had he accompanied me to an Egyptian beach resort this week he would doubtless have remarked that nothing much had changed.

Robert Hickman
Andover, Hampshire

Country living

SIR – Country pursuits feature large at my annual local ploughing match and country show. This year the committee invited ideas for a new main ring event.

"Chase a cyclist round on your tractor" was proposed but not carried.

Alan Field
Scarrington, Nottinghamshire

SIR – An entertaining alternative knob-themed event to replace the abandoned knob-eating race at Dorset's Knob Throwing Games would surely be a knobbly knees competition.

Peter Saunders
Salisbury, Wiltshire

SIR – My favourite sign seen on a village noticeboard advertising the annual fete with a display by the Red Arrows aerobatic team had across it the words: "If wet, will be held in the village hall".

Michael J. Menhenitt
Exmouth, Devon

SIR – A report submitted to an all-party parliamentary group suggested that the British countryside is a "racist colonial" space.

I sent the servants out into rural Kent yesterday to purchase a replacement safari jacket and pith helmet. Sadly they returned empty handed.

Brian Hoy
Crayford, Kent

SIR – Alarmed by reports that the countryside is racist, I set about interviewing many trees, shrubs, blades of grass, the odd farm gate and stile, and even an entire rolling hill.

I am pleased to report that none returned a single utterance of prejudice.

Bob Stebbings
Chorleywood, Hertfordshire

It's always tea time

SIR – Yesterday I asked my husband, "Did I make you a cup of tea?"

He replied patiently, "It was mentioned but I thought it was just a conversation piece."

Sally Barton
Stourbridge, Worcestershire

SIR – There is no such thing as over brewed tea. My particular favourite is weapons grade.

Mark Prior
Plymouth, Devon

SIR – Devastated to see in your survey of the nation's favourite biscuits that custard creams have been overlooked.

This can only be a conspiracy. Dark forces at work.

Mary Clarke
Marlborough, Wiltshire

A lot of what you fancy

SIR – Despite the recent dire warnings from the NHS about the dangers of eating a full Easter egg in a day, I succumbed to temptation: not only eating a full egg but also the two accompanying bars of chocolate. Despite my recklessness, I had a good night's sleep and have just successfully returned from the newsagent with a copy of the *Telegraph*. I realise, however, that I am not completely out of the woods and that I may be at risk, over the coming months, of developing a condition known as "Long Easter Egg" for which, apparently, there is no known cure.

David S. Ainsworth
Manchester

SIR – The female members of my household are strong women who normally face crises with equanimity. However, the news that turmoil in the cocoa market might make Toblerone an expensive luxury item has thrown them into the sort of panic-buying that happened with lavatory paper at the start of lockdown.

Don Philp
Worcester

SIR – When I complained to the manufacturers of a pot of beetroot kimchi that had leaked over all over my shopping, I was quickly informed that it was clearly marked to be kept in an upright position.

Where was the warning? On the bottom of the pack. Healthy eating obviously doesn't necessarily lead to common sense.

Susan Tuck
West Runton, Norfolk

SIR – As a 70+ year old I read your feature on healthy foods with interest to see what I should be eating.

However, the recommendations stopped after the seventh decade. This leads to various thoughts – are those in the eighth, ninth and tenth decades beyond redemption? Or do we need to stop eating or, worse still, are we presumed dead?

David Dunn
Malaga, Spain

SIR – My father, an inveterate prankster, used to smear mustard on the underside of the dessert spoon at dinner parties.

Philip Chandler
London N15

The steaks are high

SIR – Former *Great British Bake Off* winner David Atherton tells us that in an authentic Cornish pasty 12.5 per cent of the filling is beef and a quarter vegetables. I'm curious (and a little apprehensive) to discover what makes up the remaining 62.5 per cent of the filling.

Peter Harper
Lover, Wiltshire

SIR – A study has shattered a myth and demonstrated that cavepeople and hunter-gatherers ate more vegetables than meat. Hardly a surprise.

Animals either ran away or simply ate attacking humans – they still have this habit. Attacked vegetables stayed put and surrendered to be eaten.

John Colbert
Walsall, Staffordshire

SIR – Vegans need educating.
Have they not heard the terrible scream from a cabbage as it has its head chopped off?

Tony Meakin
Bideford, Devon

SIR – I love animals. They're delicious.

George Adams
Brading, Isle of Wight

Drinking, fast and slow

SIR – I notice that Titanic Distilleries are launching a new whiskey. Will the barman always suggest "More ice with that, sir?" – and will the toast always be "Bottoms up"?

Bruce Wilkinson
Peterborough, Cambridgeshire

SIR – Your article asks: "What does one glass of alcohol do to your body?" Not enough, if you ask me.

Robert Edwards
Hornchurch, Essex

SIR – I do not need a drink to raise my blood pressure. Looking at the newspaper and seeing what is going on in the world does it for me.

Robert Ward
Loughborough, Leicestershire

SIR – I worked out years ago what it is in red wine that gives you the headache. It's usually the second bottle.

Ian Prideaux
London SW4

Pipe down

SIR – I had a friend at school whose father was a lifelong pipe smoker.

He boasted of his father's ability to fill the bowl, strike a match, light the pipe then dispose of the match through the car window, while driving his car.

But his father stopped on the day he filled his pipe, struck the match, put it between his lips and threw the pipe out of the window.

John Sykes
Huddersfield, West Yorkshire

SIR – My late father was a pipe smoker and also a volunteer fireman in our village station. At his funeral I was chatting with his station officer who remembered a chimney fire they both attended. While they were on the roof checking that everything was properly out they noticed a distinct smell of burning cloth and plastic but couldn't see the cause... until my father turned around. "David, your trousers are on fire".

Moral of the story: don't put your pipe in your pocket, even if you are a fireman.

Tim Wright
Rampisham, Dorset

Healthy, wealthy and wise

SIR – You report on an NHS trial scheme that pays men to lose weight.

I'm classed as underweight but am now thinking of supplementing my pension by eating a few cream buns and earning a few bob for the consequences.

Tony Manning
Barton on Sea, Hampshire

SIR – My husband attended a health check-up recently and the data was recorded on his medical records. Someone had entered his height as 1.8cms instead of 1.8mtrs. Consequently his BMI read as being over 222,000. Is this a record?

Alexandra Rous
London SE23

SIR – Reading your report that GPs are worried that patients may spot errors in their medical records reminded me that some years ago I glanced at my then GP's computer screen and had to point out that I had not had both of my kidneys removed.

Phil Corrigan
St Albans, Hertfordshire

SIR – One friend recently went to his GP and got out a piece of paper, saying he had a list of seven symptoms. The GP immediately said that he could only deal with one of those things in the consultation, to which my friend replied, "Oh, I only want to talk about one thing – me!"

Lynette Johnson
Udny, Aberdeenshire

SIR – Many years ago I asked one of my patients who was feeling his age if he had any piece of equipment at home which was 80 years old and worked perfectly. "Yes," he said: "the wife".

Dr Charles Rees
Christchurch, Dorset

Following the science

SIR – "Patients treated by female doctors 'have lower chance of dying'," says your headline. If that is correct, I'm changing my doctor at once, eternal life always having been one of my ambitions.

David Crawford
Llandudno, Conwy

SIR – Your Features section seems to tell me that sleeping on my left, right, back or front is bad for me. Should I try hanging bat-like from the frame of the bedroom door?

John Newbury
Warminster, Wiltshire

SIR – In recent years I have become less inclined to mow the lawn, a mystery to me as when younger it was a source of great enjoyment. I realise suddenly my disinclination coincided almost exactly with the onset of my wife's menopause. Does this mean I have hit the mowerpause and does anyone know of a suitable hormone replacement therapy? Pro tem I've turned to dry sherry, taken orally, to treat the worst symptoms.

Kim Thonger
Collyweston, Northamptonshire

SIR – If I had suggested talking therapy to my wife during some days of the menopause, she would have thrown a frying pan at my head.

Peers M. S. Carter
Southfleet, Kent

The essential difference

SIR – There seems to be a problem these days over defining "what is a woman". There is an easy solution. According to all statistics, women live longer than men. If every man declares himself a woman then this disparity will disappear. That is unless men and women are truly different in the first place.

Dr Gerald Edwards
Glasgow

SIR – The report on Viagra's potential to prevent dementia only confirms what most women already know – that is, where most men's brains are situated.

Shirley Sweet
Tisbury, Wiltshire

SIR – I have been told many times that women are good at multitasking. I find that this is sometimes true, as long as that is the only thing that they have to do.

Patrick Smith
Great Yarmouth, Norfolk

SIR – Today my wife of over 50 years and I were discussing the promises we made when we married. I pointed out that she had promised to obey me. She responded by pointing out that I had promised to love her. We looked at each other, and decided, both of us, that she had the better deal.

Andrew F. Drummond
Andreas, Isle of Man

Active service

SIR – My local gym, which is one floor above street level, is ahead of the game in light of the latest research on stair climbing and its beneficial effect on health. I have yet to find out how they do it, but I am certain that they add one or two additional steps overnight.

Tom Stubbs
Surbiton, Surrey

SIR – People are now becoming more and more obsessed with their daily "steps" count.

I have found that gently coasting downhill at 5mph on my electric bicycle does absolute wonders for my overall tally.

Simon Cox
Brixham, Devon

SIR – Thank you for the advice to old people to lift heavy weights to keep fit. I am very old and, thanks to Cornwall County Council's decision only to collect rubbish fortnightly, I will be developing the necessary muscles.

Isobel Barker
Torpoint, Cornwall

Special operation

SIR – In another step towards a self-service NHS my wife and I have both received texts telling us to check our own heartbeat and heart rate.

I am looking forward to the next one on self-conducted bypass operations.

Michael West
Poole, Dorset

SIR – Psychologists claim that watching a horror film such as *The Shining* can help relieve pain and stress. I await the next NHS announcement that henceforth, to cut costs, anaesthetics will be replaced by your surgeon appearing at your side with an axe and announcing: "Here's Johnny!"

Martin Bastone
East Grinstead, West Sussex

SIR – While wielding my trusty mallet in the orthopaedic theatre, I did so to the rhythm of Verdi's *Anvil Chorus*.

David Nunn FRCS
West Malling, Kent

Little grey cells

SIR – My wife bought me a Rubik's cube for my 80th birthday, believing it would provide good mental exercise. While I can solve the puzzle in less time than it takes my internet service provider to answer the phone, I still can't remember where I have left my glasses.

David Rumsey
Pinner, Middlesex

SIR – You shouldn't worry if you lose your car keys, but if you find them and can't remember what they are for, then it is time to worry.

Christopher Cann
Shaftesbury, Dorset

That was a close call

SIR – Mother wanted to name my brother Stirling after Stirling Moss. Fortunately my father overruled her choice and he was named Stephen Silver.

Melanie Silver Walker
Thurstaston, Wirral

SIR – When deciding on the name for our elder daughter, who was born in April, my husband, quite unreasonably I thought, vetoed my suggestion of April May June Julie August.

Susan August
Bedford

SIR – My brother, born in early 1936, was in danger of being called Adolf until my father caught up with the news.

Hugh Johnson
Via email

SIR – The names of both the newly appointed chairman and the chief executive at NatWest seem to confirm the old adage that "good things come to those called Thwaite".

Simon Cook
Sutton, Surrey

Out of the mouths of babes

SIR – Lord Snowden's first word, "chandelier", was fitting for someone of his social station; mine, while no less polysyllabic, was more indicative of my suburban birthplace. My mother told me it was "lawnmower". This foreshadowed my one and only gardening talent.

Mike Eldridge
Falmouth, Cornwall

SIR – My very first word was "Bugger", with which I welcomed Dad home from work, having overheard Mum's reaction to hitting her thumb with a coal hammer.

Bruce Denness
Niton, Isle of Wight

SIR – As the eldest child in a good Catholic family I am assured that my first word was "Jesus". My first sentence, however, was more mundane – "Wee wee gone down the toilet".

Mary Moore
Croydon, Surrey

SIR – On being asked whether she wanted her new sibling to be a brother or sister – at the age of four and a few months before our brother's arrival – my sister announced to all present: "Actually, I'd prefer a giraffe."

Michael Cleary
York

SIR – Last week, my husband collected our three-year-old grandson from school by car.

My husband explained to him that when he was small he had to walk to school.

Our grandson replied: "Oh, weren't you worried the dinosaurs would chase you?"

Dr Dee Dawson
London N20

That'll teach them

SIR – When my brother was at boarding school he was being bullied, mainly by the theft of his tuck, so Grandma made chocolate truffles for him out of a well-known brand of chocolate laxative.

The thefts ceased.

Peter Edwards
St Brelade, Jersey

SIR – Many years ago, while another general election was in progress, my son's school class organised a mock election in which he was agent for the Monster Raving Loony Party candidate. His candidate achieved a decisive victory. Unfortunately he had to be disqualified when it was discovered that his agent, unaware of the rules against bribery, had been distributing sweets in exchange for votes.

Diana Jones
London N12

SIR – My friend Kevin at prep school didn't like PE and decided to write a note in his father's hand. It was pretty good – just a shame it was in crayon.

John Hopkins
Beckenham, Kent

SIR – During one parents' evening for my reception-age class: a parent repeated a far-fetched claim from his imaginative child and said "I always believe my child", to which my reply was, "If I always believed your child, you'd be in prison."

Eve Wilson
Hill Head, Hampshire

SIR – My son went to Bishop Wordsworth's Grammar School in Salisbury and returned home one day to inform us that if he ever became head boy, he would be allowed to wear a decorated waistcoat and more importantly be entitled to graze his goat on the school lawn.

Alas, he never required the waistcoat or the goat.

Chris Devine
Salisbury, Wiltshire

SIR – My woodwork teacher at school had the tip of a finger missing. I don't know how he lost it but it didn't fill me with confidence.

John Hopkins
Beckenham, Kent

Make the grade

SIR – When people asked how my son did in his A-levels, I would reply "he was ace". "That's very good" was the response, to which I would reply: "No – an A, a C, and an E".

John Skeeles
Hitchin, Hertfordshire

SIR – Ofsted has four so-called one-word grades. Here are four for Ofsted: Offensive, Officious, Oppressive, Outrageous.

Garry May
Haddenham, Buckinghamshire

SIR – When I was at public school back in the early 1980s we were embarking upon the introduction of girls. A new girls' house was built and in keeping with tradition it was to be named after a former Headmaster, in this instance the late W. Hoare.

Anyway, they settled for Thornbank House in the end.

Guarin Clayton
St Helier, Jersey

SIR – Marlborough College is as ever ahead of the game with Soviet-style house names that are immune to any woke criticism: A1, A2, B1, B2, B3, C1, C2 and C3.

My own house B1 was purportedly designed by the same architect who designed Pentonville jail and I always suspected he had accidentally given the builder the plans for B-wing.

Philip Wedmore
London SE24

SIR – I knew a man called Dick who became headmaster of a well-known public school. He changed his first name to Richard so that he became Richard, Head as opposed to what might have been.

George Bastin
Stroud, Gloucestershire

To a lesser degree

SIR – I recall a degree course that combined "animal studies" with musicology. My colleagues and I thought this would be the ideal qualification for running a circus.

Dr Millan Sachania
Head Master, Immanuel College
Bushey, Hertfordshire

SIR – I see that a university is offering a degree in circus performance. This should come as no surprise; many of them seem to be run by clowns.

Jeffrey Olstead
Oswestry, Shropshire

Reading, writing, reproduction

SIR – A friend told me she was a bit nonplussed when a letter from their eight-year-old boy at prep-school wrote saying he had had sex today. It transpired that he meant to write "secs", meaning second helpings.

Felicity Guille
London SW6

SIR – My two children were an academic year apart so when sex education came around, it was left to Mum (or Dad) to instruct them at the same time, using a simplified book sent from school.

I sat them down and proceeded to do the best I could and, at the end, asked if they had any questions. "Yes", said my son (aged nine), "Can I go out and play football now?". My daughter looked up from her knitting and said "Yes. Do you know how to cast off?"

I am not sure if I did a good job or not – but I do know I have five lovely grandchildren.

Margaret Scattergood
Solihull, West Midlands

SIR – While researching an O-level project on Charles Dickens back in the early 1970s, I asked my mother if she could obtain a copy of *The Victorian Underworld* by Kellow Chesney.

On requesting said book, explaining "It's for my teenage son – he is fascinated by the subject", she was a bit taken aback by the expression on the librarian's face. It turned out that she believed my mother had asked for a copy of *Victorian Underwear*.

Peter Hall
Marden, Kent

SIR – I scanned the treatise by Nick Harding on male undies with fleeting interest, until my eyes lit upon the phrase "passion killers"; whereupon I was led to consider the role of such items. I had previously assumed that underwear was an easily washable barrier between the smelly bits and the everyday clothes. When did it become a vital aid to passion?

Presumably, the Victorians and Edwardians (to name but two) had passionless intercourse in the dark with their eyes closed, merely to populate the gene pool.

Barry Sheldon
Cholsey, Oxfordshire

Brief encounters

SIR – Every year, Cheltenham race week reminds me of a love that was never to be.

On one of my regular train journeys to visit my late parents in Cheltenham, another passenger and I began flirting outrageously.

He said he always came to the festival. I was thrilled, because I liked the festival too.

Our warm friendship shrivelled when I discovered he was on about horses and he discovered I was on about literature.

Strangers on a train who never met again.

Anne Jappie
Cheltenham, Gloucestershire

SIR – I had a message seeking "friendship" from someone who said he had fallen in love with my beautiful eyes in my Facebook profile picture.

My profile picture is of my Cavalier King Charles Spaniel.

Joyce Hall
Newton-le-Willows, Lancashire

SIR – Recently one of my daughters was taken on a first date to listen to a talk given by a retired FBI agent about serial killers.

The relationship did not blossom.

Nigel Tipple
Great Coxwell, Oxfordshire

SIR – I had a boyfriend in the 1970s who had a grey parrot called Pixie. One night I went to my boyfriend's flat for a drink before he took me out to dinner. On my arrival Pixie said: "which bedroom". I left before the drink arrived.

Rosemary Corbin
Zeals, Wiltshire

SIR – According to the latest research, humans may be able to reproduce in the weightlessness of space.

It can now only be a matter of time before personnel aboard the International Space Station become members of the 227 nautical mile-high club – making the question "Did the Earth move for you?" redundant.

Nicholas Young
London W13

The modern mail

SIR – Reports that the Royal Mail is considering axing the Saturday delivery has brought dismay to many, including your correspondents.

It's not that the actual delivery will be missed – the visit of the postman on a daily basis has not occurred for quite a while now, and the world has not spun from its axis – but the news has sent my shareholding in the English Elastic Band Company into a tailspin.

Michael Latham
Oakham, Rutland

Humanity 2.0

SIR – I read with interest your article about what has happened to those children who were able to join Mensa at a very young age. I think it is notable that none have become despots or dictators or have in other ways tried to do harm to the rest of humanity.

I think this bodes well for artificial intelligence.

Julian Gall
Godalming, Surrey

SIR – The news that AI may be capable of destroying the human race is particularly distressing when you think of our respectful stewardship of the planet and the universal desire to co-exist in peaceful harmony.

Chris Nancollas
Yorkley, Gloucestershire

SIR – Elon Musk says that, in the future, AI will make going to work optional. For most people in Britain I thought it already was.

Tim Wadsworth
Malmesbury, Wiltshire

SIR – I found William Sitwell's article – "move over Fido – Voyager I shows we'll all love robots soon" – very reassuring. Up to its publication, my wife had felt my current extramarital affair with our new "robomop" Arnie to have been somewhat strange. Now I have been joined by at least one other person.

Arnie entered my life relatively recently, after a brief dalliance with my Alexa speaker was replaced with a full-on, but sadly platonic romance with a robo-carpet machine. The latter regrettably had some limitations, mainly caused by its own suicidal tendencies to crash down stairs, or bury itself in dark remote corners.

With Arnie on the scene, gone are the endless days of hoovering, before hours of fruitless mop and bucket antics.

I would certainly share a sofa with him, and he would deserve a front seat for any robo-themed movie. However, his desire to work himself to an early grave means that he hardly sits still long enough for an advertising break, let alone a feature-length movie.

Andrew Young
Olu Deniz, Fethiye, Turkey

The person you are calling is unavailable

SIR – I am of the age which qualifies me to have a place in God's waiting room.

All our financial assets are locked away on my smartphone which can only be accessed by face recognition. The question my wife and I discussed was how she was going to be able to access this vital info if I passed on suddenly.

Perhaps pickling my head, left in a glass jar with the eyes open, could do the trick.

Ramesh Nayak
Louth, Lincolnshire

SIR – While I was trying to cancel my house insurance, the music playing to keep me entertained during the long long wait on the phone was *Hotel California*: "You can check out anytime you like but you can never leave."

Somebody has a sense of humour.

Christine Tomblin
Nottingham

SIR – I was pleased to see that HMRC is planning to shut phone helplines for six months every year as this will be a significant improvement from the twelve months that is currently in place.

Trevor Saving
Sevenoaks, Kent

SIR – HMRC insists that staff working from home are held to the same standard as those in the office. We're all doomed!

Sue Milne
Crick, Northamptonshire

Computer says no

SIR – I see that Nasa has managed to put right the fault on a space probe that is 50 years old and billions of miles away. Perhaps they could help with my laptop.

Robert Pugh
Llandeilo, Carmarthenshire

SIR – Elon Musk can implant a microchip into your brain – but could he get you a GP appointment?

Michael Fabb
Chobham, Surrey

SIR – When the only automatically suggested responses to a text message asking "Are you any better?" are "Not really" and "No", I suspect that the app isn't designed for the British market.

Wouldn't "Fine, thanks", "Not too bad" or even "It's only a flesh wound" be of more use here?

Tim Barnsley
Berwick-upon-Tweed, Northumberland

SIR – I am becoming increasingly concerned about the "Big Brother" society in which we live. Today I received an email from Thames Water headlined "High Consummation Detected".

Tony Kerslake
Kingston upon Thames, Surrey

SIR – Confusion reigns here following an email from Southern Water:

"Footer content to go here dolor sit amet, consectetur adipiscing elit, sed do eiusmod tempor incididunt ut labore et dolore magna aliqua. Ut enim ad minim veniam, quis nostrud exercitation."

As clear as the water at Shoreham-by-Sea.

Alyson Persson
Henfield, West Sussex

SIR – Going online to buy a book from one of my saved sources, my automatically saved password was rejected. I entered it manually and it was still rejected, so I resorted to re-setting the password. After four attempts, all my alternative offerings were also rejected. In exasperation I entered "oh-Sodoff". This apparently was fine.

Howard Stephens
Burgh St Peter, Norfolk

Have a little faith

SIR – I am an atheist but I help my Catholic wife by polishing the brass vases for her church flower arrangements. I call it an insurance premium.

Dave Alsop
Churchdown, Gloucestershire

SIR – The following notice was posted in the entrance to a church in Copenhagen:

"When you enter a place of worship it may be possible to hear the call of God.

However it is unlikely that he will call you on your mobile phone."

John Stewart
Terrick, Buckinghamshire

SIR – I read with interest the idea of very short religious services which will allow attendance by those who cannot spare the time for a full service.

Surely even easier is "WFH", or Worship from Home.

Peter Cartledge
Tetchill, Shropshire

SIR – Having spent 42 years as a verger, serving in four English cathedrals, I have experienced a few problems involving four-legged attendees. Serving Winchester Cathedral in the 1980s we were regularly joined at evensong by a dog accompanying a lady, and by a lady who brought a cat to evensong, in a pushchair.

Likewise at Lincoln Cathedral not only were dogs welcomed by accompanied tourists and pilgrims, they occasionally were sighted at service. Mind you we had to draw the line when on one occasion a lady attended evensong with a ferret, concealed in her jacket hood, which, when the choir hit a certain note in the Magnificat, popped its head up and frightened the life out of an American tourist.

John G Campbell
Independent Funeral Celebrant & Public Speaker
Lincoln

SIR – Miss Otis, my late Jack Russell, was – and Bella my black lurcher is – a regular at church.

Bella is usually impeccably behaved except once when she gave a loud, heartfelt sigh during a long and boring sermon. The vicar said "Oh Bella, am I boring you? Quite right" and wrapped up his sermon.

The congregation was grateful.

Rosemary Coates
Apethorpe, Northamptonshire

SIR – I read with dismay the plans to hold a "Rave in the Nave" in Canterbury Cathedral.

To raise more funds will the Canterbury & District Swingers Club propose "Sripp't in the Crypt"?

Denis Durkin
Bexhill-on-Sea, East Sussex

Rolling back the years

SIR – I am 75. I am in my late middle age. I have been in this state for the last decade and will continue thus until I'm 90. I may then agree that I'm old if I want to.

Jayne Roberts
Truro, Cornwall

SIR – I have been sent a £6.25 "Rewards for Life" voucher by Holland and Barrett.

It expires on November 30. Do they know something I don't?

Phil Angell
Helston, Cornwall

Everything must go

SIR – This morning I passed a sombre building displaying a prominent notice: "'Pre-paid Funerals".

A special offer, perhaps.

James Gibson
Quorn, Leicestershire

SIR – In light of the chaos in the funeral business I've given my wife instructions to fly-tip me in a remote and peaceful location. It can't be any less dignified than the treatment that these firms are offering.

Rod Beardsell
Nantwich, Cheshire

SIR – My wife has stated that when I die she will ensure that I am 10 minutes late for my own funeral and that I am buried wearing dirty shoes, punctuality and shoe polishing being my twin obsessions.

I live in mortal fear of predeceasing her.

John H Lowe
Rossendale, Lancashire

SIR – My wife has written in her will that if she goes before me, she wants half her ashes scattered at Lords and half at Cheltenham racecourse.

She is therefore sure that I will visit her on many occasions during the year.

Patrick Fuller
Upper Farringdon, Hampshire

SIR – We satisfied my father's wishes by scattering his ashes over the Fox Hounds so that he could go hunting every day.

Ann Burnett
Richmond, Surrey

SIR – My mother had the local *Burton Daily Mail* every day and the first thing that she turned to was the obituaries to see if she knew anyone there. Upon her death we included a copy of the paper with her obituary in the coffin. She would have been so pleased to be able to read it and know someone so intimately.

Barbara Matthews
Rugeley, Staffordshire

SIR – Laughter, though slightly suppressed, was heard at the funeral of a friend when his coffin entered the church adorned with L plates that he himself had insisted on.

John Scott-Smith
Toddington, Bedfordshire

SIR – Madeline Grant writes about rituals and euphemisms often associated with death, such as *popped clogs*, *passed away*, *passed* and *saying goodbye*.

For myself I would like to be referred to as *undergoing recycling*.

John Colbert
Walsall, Staffordshire

SIR – Merseysiders have a robust approach to death, as exemplified by their famously phlegmatic response to a strike of grave-diggers and crematorium workers during the Winter of Discontent. There appeared on the gate-post leading into Anfield Cemetery the sublime chalked message: "Sunday Eleven O'Clock Hearse Boot-Sale". *Ars moriendi* at its finest.

Dr Catherine Moloney
Liverpool

SIR – Graves in village churchyards are always interesting and informative. On one visit with my wife, I asked her (in the event of our demise) if she would then like to be referred to as a "relict" of me. She was not enthusiastic.

Alan Watson
Dereham, Norfolk

SIR – My all-time favourite guitar solo is David Gilmour's on *Comfortably Numb*. I've requested this be played at my funeral, as it gives the mourners something to enjoy and describes the state I will be in.

Adrian Waller
Woodsetts, South Yorkshire

SIR – I've made a recording of me singing a verse from a very old song to be played at my For a Laugh Party aka funeral.

It's called *Good-by-ee!*

Should any of your readers like to listen to my dulcet tones before I'm gone, please feel free to contact me.

Pauline Turner
Knutsford, Cheshire

Straight down to business

SIR – Many years ago we were delighted to receive an application form in the office. Under "Occupation" the lady had answered, "Domestic Goddess" and under "Marital status" the simple truth was given, "In charge".

Richard Corfield
Heathfield, East Sussex

SIR – In that brief interlude when it seemed that Russia might be moving to a Western-style economy, I was involved in the building and staffing of a large, American-owned manufacturing plant near Moscow.

A priority was to recruit local technical staff. To this end, I interviewed a young, local female graduate. To ease her into the interview, I offered a gentle start: "Why are you here today?"

The answer came back immediately: "I am here because my mother told me to come".

To this day I regret not getting the contact details for her mother instead.

John Reynolds
Nottingham

SIR – My colleague had a novel way of preparing a shortlist of candidates to be invited for an interview. We used to receive dozens of CVs from prospective candidates, all with similar experience and qualifications for the advertised post.

He threw all the applications from the top of the stairs at home. The ones that remained on the stairs were invited for an interview. This, he said, removed any subconscious bias.

What better way?

Ramesh Nayak
Louth, Lincolnshire

Counting the pennies

SIR – Today I received a letter from the Department for Work and Pensions informing me that I will be receiving an extra 25p per week after my 80th birthday. I intend to save up for a month to buy a £1.06 stamp (first class, as befitting his position) to write to the Chancellor to thank him for his largesse. I can't make up my mind how to spend the remaining 44p. I'll let you know once I have made a decision.

Dave I'Anson
Formby, Lancashire

SIR – As an impoverished student living in London in the early 1980s, I once received my monthly bank statement where the balance, after outgoings, was just 1p. My helpful bank manager had written at the bottom, "Please don't spend it all at once."

Catherine Kidson
Bradfield, Berkshire

SIR – Your report that pro-Palestinian activists occupied Barclays bank branches needs checking. Most members of the public and customers cannot find a branch anywhere.

Ted Hawkins
Sandhurst, Berkshire

SIR – There is another, less commonly mentioned, advantage to having ready access to a physical bank branch.

Some years ago I needed to withdraw a large sum in cash to make a purchase, and was glad to be able to get it from a branch in town. I shall never forget the facial expression of the clerk who asked me, with evident disapproval, a question to the effect of whether I was intending to spend it on stolen cars, unnatural vices and slow horses. If there is no bank near me, who will be left in town to disapprove of me?

Neil Sewell-Rutter
Oxford

SIR – I think we can safely say that the only bank that is unlikely to "de bank" its clients is The Bank of Mum and Dad.

Valerie Gallard
Little Bookham, Surrey

We'll weather the weather

SIR – I have succumbed to Dry January. I've bought an umbrella.

Norman Fox
Needham Market, Suffolk

SIR – Can we please have global warming back? This arctic weather is costing me a fortune.

J. Hutchinson
Worthing, West Sussex

SIR – We have just had the wettest 18 months ever recorded. I look forward to a hosepipe ban in August.

Lee Goodall
Churchdown, Gloucestershire

SIR – In order to walk the dog this morning without freezing, I was obliged to wear a hat, thick scarf, overcoat and thermal gloves: to then read that the Met Office believes we've had an April that's been warmer than average caused me to laugh out loud. Are Met Office staff perhaps working remotely in the Bahamas?

John Mounsey
Minchinhampton, Gloucestershire

SIR – My wife knows the good spring weather has arrived when I move my beers from the garage to the fridge. They are still in the garage.

Steve Cartridge
Bolton, Lancashire

SIR – Stand by your beds. Fire extinguishers at the ready. Carry water at all times.

After a miserable winter, a very wet spring and a cold and indifferent early summer, the BBC is at it again. Tomorrow might hit 22 or 23°C. Cue panic forecasts of American weather Armageddon.

What is going on? Sounds like we are all doomed. Head for the hills.

Jeremy Nunn
Andover, Hampshire

SIR – Summer has arrived in south London. At 8.30 this morning I saw my first bare-chested tattooed roofer. Most impressive; I thought I was hardy in shorts.

John Hopkins
Beckenham, Kent

SIR – I am looking forward to the summer; it is always my favourite day of the year.

Simon Martin-Redman
Frinton-on-Sea, Essex

SIR – Yesterday, June 25, I received an email from a Cornish hotel urging me to book early for the Christmas yet to come. Perhaps not just at the moment.

Nicholas Brooking Clark
Wells, Somerset

SIR – It seems that interpreting the weather produced by AI algorithms is more akin to the art of Tarot card reading than science, although on the whole, the cartomancers seem to have a better success rate.

Liam Power
Dundalk, Co Louth, Ireland

SIR – Only 48 bin days 'til Christmas!

Roger Willatt
Lyndhurst, Hampshire

Tweet of the day

SIR – Yesterday, working on my allotment, birds were welcoming the end of winter with a chorus of cheerful song. One of these however, which I could not see, was issuing a repetitive refrain which sounded for all the world like "Putin, Putin, Putin". I have done my best to identify this avian delinquent in the *Birds of Britain and Europe*, but without success. Can any reader enlighten me, or is this a cause for concern?

Alan Quinton
Eastbourne, East Sussex

SIR – The magpies in our garden are always concealing little titbits for a later date. A recent attempt to conceal half a slice of pizza in the lawn, however, was somewhat less successful.

Andrew Pearce
London SE3

SIR – In the 1990s there was an attempt to relocate Portsmouth FC's city centre ground to a coastal site. It was discovered that the chosen area was used as a staging post by migrating birds. The club bought another piece of nearby land as a wildlife sanctuary to compensate. The planning inspector was unimpressed. "How will the birds know?" he inquired.

Mike Thomas
Brill, Buckinghamshire

SIR – In the 1950s, I had some splendid great aunts, who kept chickens and relied on them for eggs. They went off the lay and my aunts became more and more exasperated with them, until the day when one went out and gave them a lecture stating that if there were no eggs, first one and then another would be for the pot. The next day there was an egg. As my aunts did not know which hen had laid it, they were all reprieved.

Hilda Gaddum
Macclesfield, Cheshire

Hit the ground crawling

SIR – One has to wonder whether Cadbury has a secret marine sea-snail farm, considering it took the Romans 12,000 of the pesky critters to create two grams of their trademark colour purple.

N W Bainbridge
Peterborough, Cambridgeshire

SIR – The RSPCA has come under fire over an advert that suggests killing snails is cruelty to animals.

I propose a "Protect a Slug" campaign and will be quite prepared to collect up those I do not want in my garden and take them to our nearest RSPCA centre for rehoming. Maybe others would like to join my campaign?

Elizabeth Hodgson
Barnet, Hertfordshire

SIR – Last night my dog trod on a snail, crushing it to an untimely end. Should I report this to the authorities?

Michael Cattell
Mollington, Cheshire

SIR – Please reassure me that there's no truth in the rumour that car-drivers should take care not to run into flies this summer.

Margaret Stewart
Burnham-on-Sea, Somerset

SIR – This year I seem to have the usual number of bees flying blithely in through my open conservatory door, but failing to find it as a way out. I have become quite skilful with the use of a butterfly net at catching them for release outside.

How many million years of evolution will it take before insects understand the concept of glass?

Reg W. Selfe
Benfleet, Essex

Can't stop the feline

SIR – Now the Government has proved ineffective at solving the big issues, cat collars and cat flaps are the subject of debate and possible legislation. Even my cat thinks that's crazy.

Jane Holt
Falmouth, Cornwall

SIR – I see that coaxing a cat in the street could become a criminal offence under newly proposed legislation.

In my experience, some cats will not need coaxing. They recognise a mug at a distance and make a beeline for them.

Bob Paterson
Newbury, Berkshire

SIR – As anyone who has been owned by a cat will testify – you cannot coax them to do anything. Humans are merely staff.

Jane Bayly
Preston, Lancashire

Who's a clever boy?

SIR – Vets have always understood the cleverness and manipulative skills of our canine companions. I once worked with a colleague who would, fairly frequently, write "DMITO" on canine medical records. I asked what this abbreviation meant. "Ah," he said, "That stands for 'Dog More Intelligent Than Owner'."

Dr Richard Allport MRCVS
Potters Bar, Hertfordshire

SIR – As a feisty Jack Russell cross, and on behalf of all like-minded dogs, I strongly object to the current humiliating trend which refers to my fellow canines and myself as "fur babies".

It is time we took a stand.

Boris Falconer
c/o Mary Falconer
Barnet, Hertfordshire

SIR – I like well-trained dogs provided they belong to somebody else.

Dr Anthony Hawks
Clevedon, North Somerset

SIR – Have any of the correspondents complaining about dogs in hotels ever brought such joy to an establishment that they were rewarded with a free sausage and a tummy tickle?

George "Jack" Russell
c/o Malcolm Ellis
Bushey Heath, Hertfordshire

SIR – My favourite cafe displays a sign reading "Dogs welcome. People tolerated". It is regularly full.

Rupert Orr
Gravesend, Kent

SIR – As an avid reader in my younger years I was a frequent user of our library using both my husband's and my card to bring home piles of books, which were left lying around. None of them ever came to harm until our new Labrador puppy, also apparently an avid reader, selected one title from the pile and eagerly devoured it from cover to cover. I retrieved the mangled remains of *How to train your puppy* and took it back to the library, tail between my legs, cheque book in hand; the librarian roared with laughter, forgave me and excused the fine.

In all the dog's remaining 14 years she didn't so much as look at a book.

Felicity Thomson
Alloway, South Ayrshire

Dinner's in the dog

SIR – My Basset-Griffin, Alice, excelled at breaking and entering.

One of her greatest triumphs was getting into the cupboard where the cleaner left her handbag, opening said bag's zip and removing and eating the ham sandwich that had been inside. The only evidence was a neatly rolled up piece of silver foil left next to the bag – and the fact that she had forgotten to put the bag back in the cupboard.

Liz Beaumont
Via email

SIR – Over the years, our beloved chocolate Labrador has managed to help himself to an entire carved Halloween pumpkin, leaving a perfectly intact skin; the finest Swiss chocolates, hidden in a bedroom so even the intended recipient couldn't find them; a box of Harrod's luxurious, whisky-infused mince pies, the foil cases and box licked clean; my son's personalised 18th birthday cake (24 slices) – box, board and ribbon neatly left on the kitchen floor without a crumb in sight – and 1kg of dried fruit, soaking overnight, intended to be baked into a tea loaf. This is not to mention my most expensive, treasured leather boots and, of course, numerous sheepskin slippers. Any one of these could have made him extremely ill, or worse, killed him. He is currently sleeping in his bed at the ripe old age of 15 and seems none the worse for his gastronomic adventures.

Stella Currie
Bramhall, Cheshire

SIR – My parents, both teetotallers, received a splendid bottle of brandy each Christmas which was spirited away in a cupboard and forgotten. One morning, they noticed that Jacky, our budgerigar, was not his usual self. As he hadn't improved all day, my mother retrieved the hidden brandy and gave Jacky a quick nip. Sad to say, on waking the next day we found that the poor little chap "had ceased to be".

Barbara Suffolk
West Horsley, Surrey

'Tis the season

SIR – With offers from major retailers, glossy catalogues, food stores and wine merchants, it's beginning to cost a lot like Christmas.

Donald MacKenzie
Inverness

SIR – There seems to be little perfume advertised. I may buy some parfum instead, whatever that may be.

Henry Maj
Armitage, Staffordshire

SIR – Black Friday seems to be going on for an awfully long time.

Adam D. Secretan
Lewes, East Sussex

SIR – With Christmas nigh and nutcrackers at hand, let the annual man versus nut contest begin.

Edward Hill
Chandler's Ford, Hampshire

SIR – I must be on Santa's good list this year. When I took the Christmas lights from the loft, I didn't need to spend hours untangling them, as I have needed to in past years.

Chris Yates
Peasedown St John, Somerset

Card-carrying member

SIR – We have trained our Jack Russell terrier, Coco, to fetch all the post together in return for a small treat. Last December when Christmas cards began to arrive she started bringing them in one by one to increase her tally of treats. Her total stands at seven.

Chrissie Davies
Cullompton, Devon

SIR – Two years ago we sent Christmas cards produced by a charity that supports research into stammering, because stammering had resulted in a tragedy in the family of a colleague. We had several worried enquiries about which member of the family was so affected. Last year, we chose cards from MacMillan Cancer Support, because we thought it a worthy cause – result, several very concerned calls and emails. I hesitate to send RNLI cards this year, lest people think we have been shipwrecked.

Howard Stephens
Burgh St Peter, Norfolk

SIR – In view of the current and future disarray with Royal Mail I think I have come up with a cunning wheeze.

At Christmas time I shall buy my usual Christmas cards and write them out. I shall then tell all my intended recipients – by email of course – that I am not posting them because of the exorbitant cost but instead I am going to place them on my own mantelpiece. If we all do the same we shall each have our own usual colourful display of cards, the card manufacturers will stay in business and Royal Mail will learn the salutary lesson that a worsening service results in decreasing usage, until finally it disappears entirely, like water down a plughole.

Michael Turner
Winchester, Hampshire

SIR – We are going heavy on the housework before the Christmas decorations go up at the weekend. Once the tree is in place the cleaning can hold until Twelfth Night. Of course, we'll keep the place ticking over but my motto is: "See dust – Put a card on it".

Dave Alsop
Gloucester

SIR – Round robins make excellent firelighters.

Nigel Johnson-Hill
Petersfield, Hampshire

On present form

SIR – I must complain about efforts to hinder my present-distribution. I object to unswept chimneys, houses without chimneys, e-scooters, careless drivers, traffic wardens, high parking fees, congestion charges, one-way streets, ULEZ and Low Traffic Neighbourhoods.

Santa Claus
Lapland
Forwarded by:
Dr Bernard Lamb
London SW14

SIR – I recall a Christmas when I was at a boyfriend's family's Christmas lunch.

One of the children had been given a drum. In the hiatus between drinks and the call to lunch, I seized the opportunity to take the drum, crossed the farmyard, and threw the offending drum as hard as I could up into the hay loft. No one searched more diligently than I later for the missing drum.

Cherry Tugby
Warminster, Wiltshire

SIR – My husband has a very generous but somewhat chaotic approach to Christmas presents. One year, with great expectations, I unwrapped a very large box. Imagine my delight when I discovered his gift to be 100 incontinence pads. The box had appeared on our doorstep and he had decided to wrap it without further ado. I can only imagine that the nursing home next door was less delighted to find that they were 100 incontinence pads down.

Hayley Brewis
Bury St Edmunds, Suffolk

SIR – I knew I was onto a good thing when my then wife-to-be bought me a meat cleaver for Christmas.

I'm pleased to report that twelve years later, I still have both.

Adam Herrick
Sawston, Cambridgeshire

SIR – I spoiled my wife with that mother of all gifts, a wooden toilet seat.

She was delighted.

Ian Wearing
Welwyn, Hertfordshire

Come all ye tasteful

SIR – My preferred recipe for a turkey Christmas dinner is to leave the poor tasteless thing on the farm to enjoy the rest of its life and buy a goose instead.

David Barnett
Long Bennington, Lincolnshire

SIR – Why, a few years after Brexit, are we still eating Brussels sprouts?

Malcolm Freeth
Bournemouth, Dorset

SIR – Instead of receiving 1kg of sprouts, I found one free-range sprout in my Sainsbury's delivery. It was carefully labelled with a sticky till price of 0.01p. The label was bigger than the sprout. I enjoyed it.

Elizabeth Hawkins
Ventnor, Isle of Wight

SIR – If you want to know what the correct portion size is for sprouts, you have only to ask my grandchildren.

Huw Wynne-Griffith
London W8

SIR – Imagine my surprise when visiting the Seasonal Products section of my local Waitrose this morning (December 28) to see unwanted Christmas items being replaced by Easter Eggs.

What happened to the season of detoxification and all those kale-based products my wife and her friends need to consume in January?

Hedley Walls
Cirencester, Gloucestershire

A YEAR IN POLITICS

Honoured, I'm sure

SIR – Following the publication of the New Year's Honours List it is sad to see that the Crony Virus is still active.

John England
Tonbridge, Kent

SIR – Some people in the New Year's Honours List would not even qualify for a CDM (Cadbury's Dairy Milk).

Bernard Powell
Southport, Cheshire

SIR – I was informed by a contemporary that last March I was eligible for an OBE which surprised me greatly. He then explained that it stood for "Over Blooming 80" – although he used slightly stronger language.

Keith Burgess-Clements
Maidstone, Kent

SIR – It appears knighthoods are given to the minstrels and jesters rather than the warriors these days.

Victor Tee
Kintbury, Berkshire

SIR – Now that Archbishop Welby and Jilly Cooper have both received gongs in the New Year Honours, might Dame Jilly be inspired to write a clerical bonkbuster? I'm sure it would be eagerly anticipated.

Jane Moth
Stone, Staffordshire

SIR – I once saved a penalty in a football match and, regrettably, I have told many people to f— off. Please may I have a gong?

Mark Smythe
Chislehurst, Kent

A plague on both your Houses

SIR – I was intrigued to read that pest control firms were summoned to attend the House of Commons no fewer than 541 times in the 13-month period to December 2023. Sitting here, it occurs to me that they do not appear to be doing a particularly good job. Allowing for the usual handful of absentees, the building is still overrun with well over 600 of them.

Nick Metcalfe
Bramhall, Cheshire

SIR – Mother of Parliaments? Looks like the parent in question went out to do some shopping and left the infants in charge.

Jon Price
Upton, Wirral

Ups and downs on Downing Street

SIR – May I suggest that the present door to No 10 be replaced by a revolving version?

Gerry Doyle
Liverpool

SIR – Having watched all the comings and goings at No 10 I have come to the conclusion that what is needed more than ever is a porch. It must be freezing inside when the wind's blowing, and I bet they haven't got a heat pump.

Nick Tracken
St Neots, Cambridgeshire

SIR – Beyond the political arguments of Suella Braverman's sacking, I for one have some empathy for her. She was sacked twice from the same post in little over a year.

I was myself sacked twice from the same post, as captain of the local pub cricket team. My overall record as skipper read:

Played Four, Lost Four, Sacked Twice.

A hasty reinstatement after my first three games was considered ill-judged, so I was promptly dismissed again.

Ralph Herson
London NW1

SIR – It really is amazing to hear that as soon as a Cabinet minister has left office they have all of the answers to solve all the major problems that they failed to deal with when they were in office.

Brian Storey
Cambridge

SIR – A new word for the Oxford English Dictionary, "Cleverly", defined as "not being too smart".

Stuart Geddes
Monmouth

SIR – I welcome an MP who is openly gay, especially one good at his job. I do have concerns when an MP appears to be openly stupid.

Alan France
Marlow, Buckinghamshire

SIR – Having watched *Johnny English* tonight I am convinced that it is the basis of the present governance of this fine country.

Michael Knight
Taunton, Somerset

SIR – A duty of candour is a very good idea. However, for politicians to vote for a duty of candour for other people is a bit like a Thieves' Kitchen urging other people to stop nicking stuff.

Derek McMillan
Durrington, West Sussex

Fighting the Speaker's corner

SIR – If Sir Lindsay Hoyle has upset both the Tories and the SNP, then he must be doing something right.

Roy Bailey
Great Shefford, Berkshire

SIR – I am Mr Peaker and I know I could do a decidedly better job as Mr Speaker. Where does one apply?

Mark Peaker
London W1

Back where we started

SIR – I fear that Larry the cat is very confused by the reappearance of David Cameron in Downing Street. Actually, I think most of us share that confusion.

Jane Moth
Stone, Staffordshire

SIR – For me the most illustrious resident of Chipping Norton will always be Ronnie Barker, who ran an antiques shop in the town after his retirement.

Alun Harvey
Groningen, The Netherlands

SIR – I do hope that David Cameron gives Rishi Sunak the name of his tailor.

D J Harrop
Macclesfield, Cheshire

SIR – I managed my son's football team for 10 years. We made some changes over the years; some left, some were brought in. I can't remember ever ringing up the parent of a boy who left because he was utterly useless and saying "actually we're really missing a centre forward".

Christian Froggatt
Reigate, Surrey

SIR – I can only assume that Michael Portillo was unavailable to take up the post of Foreign Secretary.

Julia Clayton
Southport, Cheshire

It's the economy, stupid

SIR – The *Business Newsletter* for January 23 reports that government borrowing was £6.3bn or around 44 per cent lower than expected by forecasting "experts". Given the chasm between official forecasts and reality, isn't it time this vital task was handed over to Mystic Meg and her fellow crystal ball gazers at the next village fete? I'm sure they'd do a better job.

Iain Duffin
Crudwell, Wiltshire

SIR – The Governor of the Bank of England, Andrew Bailey, said in his response to recent criticisms that "I don't do hindsight".

It appears he doesn't do foresight either.

John Howard
Birmingham

SIR – I sometimes feel quite cheerful and then I remember that Jeremy Hunt was in charge of the NHS for seven years until just before Covid struck.

Brian Farmer
Braintree, Essex

SIR – Where will Jeremy Hunt figure on the Nigel Lawson Richter Scale? On current form, a cotton bud falling from a table.

Rod Mccarron
Porthleven, Cornwall

SIR – No money for the defence budget, thanks Mr Hunt. Will we have money in the education budget to teach us to say hello in Russian?

Michael Walford
Aldeburgh, Suffolk

SIR – The Budget can best be summed up by the words I recently noted on a car sticker which said: "Don't steal; the Government doesn't like competition".

Hugh Corrance
Westerham, Surrey

SIR – What happened to all the white rabbits?

Dr Tim Davey
Bristol

SIR – Deckchairs untouched, but a realignment of the little drinks' tables.

Geoff Hunt
Coulsdon, Surrey

SIR – We can't possibly understand the impact of the Budget until Gary Lineker has spoken.

Mike Edwards
Via email

SIR – As a pensioner, I would rather have a reduction in my tax bill now, than after I'm dead. Shrouds have no pockets.

Mike Crowe
Cullompton, Devon

SIR – Jeremy Hunt says there is light at the end of the tunnel for the economy. Unfortunately it is from a Labour train coming down the tracks driven by a well-paid unionised driver.

Christopher Hunt
Swanley, Kent

Tired old Tories

SIR – The Conservative Party has become a church so broad the roof has caved in.

Michael MacPhee
Via email

SIR – This morning I have received an email from the Conservative Party offering me 25 per cent off all mugs. What do they take us for? Mugs?

Simon Chalwin
Shaftesbury, Dorset

SIR – I have received an email from *Which?* Campaigns headlined "We want a Fraud Minister".

While I am sure they are right I did think that if we haven't had one before we will certainly have several in the very near future.

Brian Donaldson
Orrell, Lancashire

SIR – There is a danger that the new political movement PopCon (Popular Conservatism), like its near namesake popcorn, makes a lot of noise but lacks any real substance.

Mike Fowler
Princes Risborough, Buckinghamshire

SIR – The Conservative Party should include in their upcoming party election manifesto the intention to establish a Ministry of Common Sense with powers to veto blindly silly policy decisions.

Readers invited to submit examples.

Jeremy Hawke
Arundel, West Sussex

SIR – I am still going to vote for the Conservatives at the next general election. It's just that they've changed their name to Reform UK.

Adrian Davies
Huddersfield, West Yorkshire

SIR – We are now well on course to a large Labour Party majority at the next general election. The Tory Party has dug the country's grave; the Labour Party will fill it in. It is then just a case of who puts what on the tombstone.

Ian Jenkins
Hereford

SIR – It used to be said that the Church of England was the Tory Party on its knees. It is perhaps ironic that, as the Church seems to be on its last legs, the Tory Party is indeed on its knees.

Richard Iley
Birmingham

Sext scandal

SIR – The revelations concerning the MP William Wragg shed some much-needed light on the term "Politically Exposed Person".

Dermot Burke
Farnham, Surrey

SIR – Maybe the Government should rethink any plans it has on restricting smartphone ownership by teenagers. I suggest that this could be extended to include MPs and even possibly employees of the Civil Service.

Philip Samengo-Turner
Cirencester, Gloucestershire

Notional health chief

SIR – Rarely seen in 2023, I wish to report the first sighting in 2024 of Amanda Pritchard earlier this week.

Stephen Howey
Woodford Green, Essex

SIR – Does Amanda Pritchard exist?

Malcolm Guy
Keighley, North Yorkshire

SIR – The NHS is to declare that sex is a matter of biology, says your report.

Goodness me – now that someone with more than one brain cell is reviewing the NHS, things are looking up.

Dudley Price
Wells, Somerset

Is anyone here a doctor?

SIR – (Best read in a David Attenborough voice)

"Good evening.

In this special report, I want to tell you about a particular animal, native to the UK, which is in great danger of extinction. The loss of this animal has serious implications for the survival of our own species.

This now shy and retiring creature, once commonly found in the UK, has become less and less visible in recent years, with evidence to show that many have migrated to richer habitats. A rare sighting in Devon a month ago has confirmed that, although some do still exist, they are unlikely to be in sufficient numbers to secure the survival of humanity in that area in particular.

That is because the primary function of this creature is to seek out and destroy as many early threats to the health of mankind as it can, using its unique abilities to directly access information in a face-to-face encounter.

I am talking about the elusive 'GP'. While it is true that subspecies, such as the NP (nurse practitioner) and the RP (receptionist) have been trying to fill in the gaps, those efforts are themselves being hampered by the arrival of a completely new species, the 111.

We must make the conservation of the GP our priority. Sightings should be reported and careful and regular monitoring visits made. The 111 should be returned to its natural Whitehall habitat, or I really do fear for the future of us all."

Chris Evans
Seaton, Devon

SIR – I have a doctor's appointment for next Thursday. I am thinking of putting it on eBay.

Steve Cartridge
Bolton, Lancashire

SIR – Does the article "GP struck off after having sex with multiple women at his surgery in working hours", with one complainant feeling she was "used as a 'sex object' to relieve his boredom", rather question the usual assertion that GPs are overworked?

Elizabeth Edmunds
Hassocks, West Sussex

No smoke without ire

SIR – Isn't it fitting that Rishi Sunak's unconservative attempt to restrict the sovereignty of free will by trying to ban smoking is coming at the fag end of this Conservative Government?

David McCarthy
Dacre Banks, North Yorkshire

SIR – What date does Prohibition start?

Jean O'Keefe
Heywood, Lancashire

SIR – Going by Rishi Sunak's attempt to be "down with the kids" by wearing Adidas Sambas, I assume smoking will soon become de rigueur with the same cohort he's trying to influence.

David McCarthy
Harrogate, West Yorkshire

SIR – As teenagers are contrarians by design, perhaps we should be encouraging them all to smoke.

Geraldine Wills
Chaffcombe, Somerset

SIR – A teenage reason to smoke has been its perceived ability to make you appear older. Thanks to the proposed legislation it will now do so by law.

Adam Marshall
Sorrento, Perth, Western Australia

SIR – I am thinking about having a cinnamon bun and latte tomorrow. Do I need the Prime Minister's approval?

Mark Peaker
London W1

SIR – I gave up smoking voluntarily at the age of 9, having bought 10 Woodbines in collusion with a mate. Not daring to take them home, we smoked the lot down at an air raid shelter. Suffice to say, the resultant effect ensured that 80 years later I have never touched a fag since. Although an effective way of achieving the Government's aim, I would suggest that theirs is a more acceptable method to improving the nation's health in the long term.

Ron Giddens
Caterham, Surrey

SIR – If ever the smoking bill becomes law, the very next day I propose to establish the Church of the Noble Smoke Pixie, a religion to which entry is only available to those born after 2009.

It will be an unspoken requirement of the faith that all adherents undertake to purchase cigarettes when they wish and that, on a number of occasions throughout each day, they may light and smoke some of those in honour of the venerated Smoke Pixie. This is an essential demonstration of commitment to the religion and failure to undertake the requirements will lead to excommunication to the unspeakable Hades of the health fascists, a fate worse than anything the Spanish Inquisition ever enacted in their time.

There will be no cost for membership of the Church of the Noble Smoke Pixie; membership will be freely available to anyone in the defined age-range without any discrimination or formal process. That seems to work for the others.

The new law will, of course, not apply to the pursuit of religious requirements, clearly deserving similar freedom to that awarded to other religions with regard, for example, to the carrying of blades and the wearing of certain items of clothing.

All praise the Noble Smoke Pixie, coming soon to a teenager near you.

Graham Hoyle
Cradley, Herefordshire

Both sides now

SIR – I read with interest that scientists have discovered that faces can reveal your political leanings. I've wondered what happens when you change your allegiance. I await the moment when Dan Poulter's face drops.

Martin Bastone
West Grinstead, West Sussex

SIR – I have waited patiently for the Conservatives to reveal their winning strategy for clinching the next general election.

Defection to the Labour Party was not quite what I had in mind.

Martyn Pitt
Gloucester

SIR – If things carry on in the same way as they have over the last couple of weeks, Sir Keir Starmer is going to have to create a lot more peers.

Patrick Evershed
London SW1

SIR – I have a plan for the Tories to win the next election. I suggest that all Conservative MPs defect to the Labour Party (don't worry they're not fussy) and win their seats wearing red rosettes. Then the day after the election they can defect back again.

Oh, wait. They're ahead of me.

Tom Harris
Reigate, Surrey

SIR – Every time a Conservative MP crosses the floor to Labour, it raises the average IQ of both parties.

Richard Skaife
Shaftesbury, Dorset

Left behinds

SIR – Following George Galloway's characterisation of Rishi Sunak and Keir Starmer as two cheeks of the same backside, I was relieved that he didn't locate Ed Davey.

Andrew Shuttleworth
Saffron Walden, Essex

SIR – The good news is that within the year George Galloway will be history. I can't wait.

Richard Cavendish
Ashburton, Devon

SIR – Why anyone would vote for a man who pretended to be a cat on national television is beyond me.

Michael Bristow
Bristol

Ex-prime-minister-in-waiting

SIR – I am enjoying your photographs of Rishi Sunak trying out various apprenticeships. He seems to show such enthusiasm and no doubt this will give him a head start when he visits his local Job Centre after the general election. Having reviewed this week's selection of pictures I think I would be happy for him to become a television cameraman, but not sure I want him to rewire my home. However, I wish him well in his endeavours.

William T Nuttall
Rossendale, Lancashire

SIR – We really are a throwaway society. Look how we treat prime ministers.

Field McIntyre
London SW3

SIR – If any Tory MPs seriously think of changing to a new prime minister, then maybe it's simpler to say all remaining Tory MPs will each become PM for one day to avoid arguments. Maybe in alphabetical order of surnames.

Dan Hartley
Solihull

SIR – In *Monty Python*, The Black Knight vows to fight on, despite losing all his limbs ("I'll bite your legs off!").
Rishi Sunak sounds more and more like him every day.

Rupert Godfrey
Heytesbury, Wiltshire

SIR – If the Prime Minister is in need of ideas to help boost his chances, the *Telegraph* Letters Page would be a good place to start.

Steve Scarlett
East Barsham, Norfolk

Take me to our leader

SIR – If AI is as advanced as we are led to believe, can we bring back Margaret Thatcher?

Nigel Algar
Bottesford, Nottinghamshire

SIR – Liz Truss had all the right ideas, but in the wrong order.

John McLaren
Farnham, Surrey

SIR – I think Sir Billy Connolly should be made honorary prime minister.

At least he would cheer us up.

Anthony Clark
Kendal, Cumbria

SIR – I am intrigued by the possibility of Boris "shopping trolley" Johnson returning to the fray. I wonder if he will be getting a new set of wheels attached first. Ones capable of following a consistent course for more than about two minutes.

Michael Oak
Stirling

SIR – I had a dream: a new political party with true Conservative beliefs led by Nigel Farage, Liz Truss, Suella Braverman, John Hayes and Lord Frost.

Then I awoke and it was still grey and raining.

Grenville Edwards
Albaston, Cornwall

SIR – Frost/Farage/Johnson might make an excellent Triumvirate. Any one of them could be Caesar, but he would have to take his holidays in March.

Neale Edwards
Chard, Somerset

SIR – I was not at all surprised to read that Penny Mordaunt was voted by Tory councillors as the MP who would make the best leader. My question is who the hell did they find to make up the other five names on the shortlist?

Richard Smedley
Newark, Nottinghamshire

SIR – I understand Penny Mordaunt's desire not to be "installed like a new boiler", but having had a new one fitted this week, I can say that it is reliable and cost-effective, unlike its predecessor.

Rachael Soul
Witney, Oxfordshire

SIR – My late wife was a primary school teacher.
I think she would have been very well qualified to run the present Conservative Party.

Alastair Mutch
Kendal, Cumbria

SIR – Is there any chance of Rishi Sunak recalling Sir Robert Peel to government?
Something needs to be done about the surge in shoplifting.

Bob Harvey
Oxted, Surrey

Party animals

SIR – It is not only the human electorate that has grown tired of government incompetence and Opposition ineffectiveness. Larry the Mouser at Downing Street for the past thirteen years has been privy to all Cabinet meetings and all the Covid intrigues. Of course his patriotism and total discretion are not in doubt because he wears a Union Flag bow tie. Foreign leaders respect his authority and even President Trump's limo waited to leave while Larry dozed under it. Our own wise feline George has held talks with Larry and advises that Larry and numerous loyal felines remain on standby for a call from Clarence House should the King seek the services of the Cats Reform Party.

John Pritchard
Ingatestone, Essex

SIR – Dogs might be man's best friend. However: the power lies with cats.

On the evening 10 o'clock news on January 11, while the reporter was in full flow reporting from in front of 10 Downing Street, Larry nonchalantly strolled up to the door. A quick lick of his paws and a stroke of the whiskers, the door was opened, and in he walked.

I still have no idea what the reporter was saying.

Bernard Clark
Sedgeford, Norfolk

SIR – I was sitting in the garden today watching our cat. She walked along the fence and then sat down and appeared to sleep. I thought perhaps she should stand for election.

Tony Scofield
Glastonbury, Somerset

SIR – In the past we have seen an octopus predicting the outcome of the World Cup, so this year why not use the renowned sagacity of our feline friends to predict the general election result?

All we will need are two identical bowls of the same cat food, one painted blue and one red. These would be placed equidistant from the front door of 10 Downing Street and Larry would then be released to make his choice.

No need for endless TV and radio debates.

I commend the idea to the nation.

Colin G. Parker
Thame, Oxfordshire

The agony of choice

SIR – I intend to vote at the general election; out of duty not conviction. However, I feel the choices available are like being asked if I would prefer to be savaged by a lion or tiger.

B.N. Bosworth
Blakedown, Worcestershire

SIR – I hope the forthcoming election will be soon. Every time the word is mentioned on the radio or television, Alexa kicks off.

Nairn Lawson
Portbury, Somerset

SIR – The lady ticking off lists of names at Thursday's local elections gave me a long strange look before asking if I had any other form of identification. I had mistakenly given her my Costco membership card.

Camilla Coats-Carr
Teddington, Middlesex

SIR – I've decided where to put my cross on polling day. It will go to whichever party promises to get rid of this awful weather we're currently experiencing.

Ann Wright
Cambridge

Things can only get wetter

SIR – How I sympathise with our Prime Minister; standing out in the rain to announce the forthcoming election.

I hope neither he, nor his party, shrink.

Mark Hodson
Bristol

SIR – So now we know how Rishi gets his suits to fit so snugly. I remember lying in the bath in my first pair of Levi 501s to achieve a similar effect.

Audrey Lindsay
Peover Superior, Cheshire

SIR – Sunak: the wally without a brolly.

Peter Flesher
Halifax, West Yorkshire

SIR – It may have been wallpaper for Boris, but it's definitely curtains for Rishi.

Giles Rowe
Dunsany, Co. Meath, Ireland

SIR – Rishi Sunak may believe that his plan is working. Unfortunately, it's the wrong plan.

Roger Simmens
Lyndhurst, Hampshire

SIR – With all the Tory Party election claims that "we have a plan", I wouldn't be surprised if one of them were to employ Baldrick of *Blackadder* fame as their Special Adviser.

George Sabiniak
Writtle, Essex

SIR – Rishi Sunak's request to the King for permission to dissolve Parliament could be the best thing he has done. Once "dissolved" it (Parliament) can be flushed down the drains and discharged into the sea, by the water companies, with all the other effluent.

Eric Parkman
Eastbourne, East Sussex

Labour pains

SIR – Rachel Reeves' claim that Labour would usher in a decade of "national renewal" is interesting. However, given the condition of the body national, perhaps "revival" may be a more appropriate word.

Stuart Ashton
Whitley Bay, Northumberland

SIR – No-one should be concerned about higher CGT bills should Labour be elected to power. Their plans for the economy mean no-one will have a CG on which to pay higher T.

Bob Lyddon
Wells-next-the-Sea, Norfolk

SIR – I understand that Sir Keir Starmer, if elected to power, proposes to renegotiate with the EU to improve Brexit outcomes for the UK. I'll have a pint of whatever he's drinking.

Ian Thompson
Ingst, South Gloucestershire

SIR – Is the Leader of the Opposition following in the steps of Groucho Marx? To paraphrase: "These are my policies, and if you don't like them ... Well, I have others."

Graham W. Swift
Newcastle-under-Lyme, Staffordshire

SIR – Despite Sir Keir Starmer being dusted in glitter by some eco fairy, I suspect it highly unlikely we shall see any magic.

Michael Johnston
Oxted, Surrey

SIR – Sir Keir Starmer wishes to lower the voting age.

Sixteen is far too young to consent to be screwed over in a polling booth.

Edward Hill
Chandler's Ford, Hampshire

SIR – Does the Labour Party have any exciting ideas or will the whole manifesto be about banning things that are already illegal?

Edward Church
Selling, Kent

SIR – Given the volume of laxatives dispensed by the NHS, I'm disappointed that "Getting Britain Moving" isn't Labour's strategy for constipation.

Michael Heaton
Warminster, Wiltshire

SIR – Labour will soon be unveiling some new policies.

Keir Starmer has just bought the whole box set of *Yes Minister*.

Denis Tucker
Dinas Powys, Vale of Glamorgan

SIR – How long can Sir Keir Starmer go on making keynote speeches without a keynote?

Peter Boxall
Haddenham, Buckinghamshire

SIR – Please could Sir Keir Starmer explain where his levers of growth are, and why no-one else has found them, without resorting to more cliches?

Clive Henly
Chippenham, Wiltshire

SIR – I thought Starmer said he had no problem with being ruthless. Perhaps I misread it and it actually said *toothless*.

Geoff France
Holmfirth, West Yorkshire

SIR – I feel sorry for Sir Keir Starmer for making a mistake while under pressure in a live interview and saying that he had two sons, when in fact he has a son and a daughter.

The error will be quickly forgotten by most of us, but if his children are anything like mine, the poor man will be teased about it for the rest of his life.

Julian Ellis
Fiskerton, Northamptonshire

Rise of the red queen

SIR – Fraser Nelson says that people find it hard to get terrified by Sir Keir Starmer.

They should remember that his deputy is Angela Rayner. That should do the trick.

Guy Bargery
Edinburgh

SIR – The deputy leader of the Labour Party is trying to mirror Monty Python's four Yorkshiremen, who were vying to outdo each other with how poor they were growing up.

Perhaps she had to get up an hour before she went to bed to sweep the factory floor.

Bill Todd
Whitton, Middlesex

SIR – As Jeremy Corbyn was one of the Tory Party's greatest assets at the last general election, and as Angela Rayner is now sharing that role, the last thing they should wish for is her to quit as Labour deputy leader.

Brian Christley
Abergele, Conwy

SIR – Angela Rayner says Labour will build a new generation of Milton Keynes-style towns. I have been to Milton Keynes; if anything is worth keeping Labour out of power, it is the promise of more.

Andrew Pearce
London SE3

SIR – It occurs to me that frequent appearances by Emily Thornberry could be the Conservatives' best chance of winning the general election.

Michael Tyce
Waterstock, Oxfordshire

Who governs Britain?

SIR – I note that our prime-minister-in-waiting wishes to stop work at 6pm on Friday in order to spend more time with his family.

I am one of a group of four "mature" gentlemen who have met every Thursday for the best part of 30 years to discuss politics (yes, our respective spouses continue to despair). We have a wide range of political allegiances but nonetheless we have agreed to put our differences aside and band together for the sake of the nation to offer our services to Sir Keir Starmer on a job-share basis. We appreciate that our part of the job will have long hours (6pm through to 9am daily and also weekends) but we are up for this. We stand ready.

Jim Prentice
Stirling

SIR – Sir Keir Starmer has suggested that he plans to clock off as PM at six o'clock on a Friday. On the plus side, that will give our armed forces a clue about when Putin's invasion will come.

Martin Smith
Brimpsfield, Gloucestershire

SIR – Has Sir Keir indicated who will be the Minister for Levelling Down when he takes over?

Jeremy Douglas-Jones
Swansea

SIR – The country is in great need of a safe and sensible pair of hands. At the upcoming election, perhaps Sir Keir could be encouraged to stand aside and allow J.K. Rowling to stand in his place.

Jennie Gatheral
South Luffenham, Rutland

SIR – I would like to offer my congratulations to the Labour Party on its recruitment of Harry Potter to the Department for Education, a master stroke. How otherwise will they be able to magic up thousands of extra teachers?

Dr Martin Stephen
Cambridge

SIR – Won't it be wonderful when Labour is in Government and everything in this country will be run or organised so superbly.

I will now take my tongue out of my cheek.

Jean Martin
Cranleigh, Surrey

SIR – Please may I have a cutting from Labour's money tree?

Anne Senneck
Mere, Wiltshire

SIR – The picture of Sir Keir Starmer selling ice cream caused much mirth in this household. We felt working in a patisserie might be more apt, selling the limited edition "Labour 24" offering of fruitcakes mixed with nuts.

Tim Rann
Mirfield, West Yorkshire

That's enough, Ed

SIR – From observing the antics of Ed Davey et al, I am wondering whether he represents the Liberal Democrats or the Monster Raving Loony Liberal Democratic Party.

Mark S. Davies FRCS
Chipping Norton, Oxfordshire

SIR – Is Ed Davey auditioning for Bertram Mills or Parliament?

He is quite unsuited to either.

Tim Mathias
Cardiff

SIR – Ed Davey seems to be challenging the notion that there is no thing such as bad publicity.

Roger Cousins
Beaconsfield, Buckinghamshire

SIR – Presumably, should the Lib Dems win more seats than the Tories and become the official opposition, Ed Davey will confront Keir Starmer at Prime Minister's Questions while bouncing up and down on a pogo stick.

Mike Adams
Defford, Worcestershire

SIR – I feel reassured to know that when Sir Ed Davey jumps out of his canoe and into power he is going to fix the NHS, the economy and everything else in sight. I'm left wondering how he will fill his time on the second day at No 10. Canoeing on the Thames, I suppose.

Mick Ferrie
Mawnan Smith, Cornwall

The body politic

SIR – Having been given a diagnosis of breast cancer a few weeks ago, I decided to rename my boobs Starmer (firmly on the left) and Sunak (sitting on the right).

I was originally told Starmer had to go but Sunak could remain in place for another term. Now I am advised that they need to be subjected to months of chemotherapy and then both given the chop.

If only the same fate could befall their political namesakes. It would make this whole ghastly cancer business seem worthwhile.

Judi Cristalia Bennett
Watchet, Somerset

Place your bets

SIR – Craig Williams, Rishi Sunak's aide, said he made a grave error of judgement by placing £100 at 5/1 on the date of the general election. He certainly did. I got 7/1 at Paddy Power.

Dave Pibworth
Clifton Reynes, Buckinghamshire

SIR – It is no wonder that so many Conservatives had a bet on the election date to try and generate some cash. They are going to be out of work for a long time.

Chris Sparrow
Oxford

Election blues

SIR – In my work as a chartered surveyor and estate agent I was always aware of and complied with the Property Misdescriptions Act.

I feel there should be a Political Misdescriptions Act as the Conservative Party is certainly not currently Conservative.

John Marsh
Sheringham, Norfolk

SIR – There is a sad lack of bumble bees and Tories this summer.

Gilly Deane
Tisbury, Wiltshire

SIR – I do not see what all the fuss is about not having a Conservative government after the next general election. We don't have a Conservative government now.

David Wilson
Cottingham, East Yorkshire

SIR – You report that analysis suggests Sir Keir Starmer will condemn the Tories to their worst election performance since 1906. I would suggest that the Tories have done that all on their own.

Emma-Louise Bowers
London SW11

SIR – Last night three suspicious looking characters were observed prowling around our village at 3am.

It has been suggested that they were probably Tory canvassers hoping to find nobody awake.

Ken Jones
Hambledon, Hampshire

SIR – Not sure how to vote – my MP canvassed my support wearing a forage cap and a T-shirt proclaiming "got the T-shirt".

Roger Fowle
Chipping Campden, Gloucestershire

SIR – Our grandson, aged 17, wrote to each candidate in their constituency saying he was an ardent supporter and please could they send him a poster so he could promote them. Two responded. Their house is near the station car park. Commuters must be confused, if they have noticed, because each day he is swapping the posters.

Eileen Fawdry
Hampton, Middlesex

SIR – Now that we are all signed up for "saving the planet", wouldn't it be a good idea if all the electioneering propaganda was printed on toilet tissue so that it would have, at least, one use?

Greig Bannerman
Frant, East Sussex

Ch-ch-ch-changes

SIR – Labour has adopted "Change" for the election campaign.

With Starmer's huge number of U-turns and policy changes, wouldn't "short changed" be more appropriate?

Tim Jackson
Gullane, East Lothian

SIR – Although Labour is using the slogan "Change" to badge its election campaign, nowhere on the graphics does it appear to specify "for the better".

Michael Oakey
Horsham, West Sussex

SIR – If Labour wins the general election all we will have left is change.

Gregory Porter
London W8

SIR – Looking at shots of the latest Labour Big Bus highlights I was struck by the prominent position of the Lady in Red conveniently in front of the slogan so that all we read was "ANGE". Upstaging or what?

Valerie Hardwick
Ludlow, Shropshire

Talking heads

SIR – Having watched the first televised debate, I would strongly advise Sir Keir to duck the next one on the basis he is too busy washing his hair that day.

Go well it did not.

Idris White
Sevenoaks, Kent

SIR – Just before I fell asleep during the Sunak/Starmer debate, I thought to myself "Why does Keir Starmer part his hair on the wrong side?"

Derek Long
Sheffield, South Yorkshire

SIR – Forget Rishi Sunak and Keir Starmer: a three-cornered debate between Nigel Farage, Jeremy Corbyn and George Galloway would be a lot more entertaining.

Roger Jackson
Stockport, Cheshire

SIR – The conduct of last night's "debate" leads one to conclude that British democracy has been reduced to a pathetic squabble between a low wattage Max Headroom and a Norman Wisdom without the panache.

David Campbell
Bishop Auckland, Co Durham

SIR – To quote my three-year-old granddaughter (Maisie), I just wish they would "stop wording at me".

Alison Sangster
Liverpool

SIR – During the current election campaign, party leaders have been relentless in drawing our attention to the very ordinariness of their ancestry. None however has come close to ex Roxy Music guitarist Phil Manzanera's parentage; apparently, "Mummy was an asteroid, Daddy was a small non-stick kitchen utensil".

Peter Hall
Tonbridge, Kent

SIR – Normally when men remove jackets and ties and roll up shirt sleeves, some physical work is about to be done. When politicians are so attired all they seem to do is point at things.

Patrick Cleary
Nottingham

Now Sunak's sunk

SIR – Supported by untold numbers of men and women, thousands of the bravest boys and men jumped into the sea on D-Day, thus ensuring our freedom. We now have a Prime Minister who did not want his ankles splashed.

Peta Vick
Lytham St Annes, Lancashire

SIR – Even Malcolm Tucker wouldn't be able to come up with a spin to save Rishi from this latest Tory self-mutilation.

Gordon Breslin
Beckenham, Kent

They think it's all over

SIR – Gordon Rayner suggests a decent run by England's footballers in the Euros may induce a feelgood factor around the general election, to the benefit of the Conservatives. If that is indeed part of Mr Sunak's thinking, with his luck he has surely just put the kiss of death on their chances.

David Stanley
London SW6

SIR – I'm already wishing that Rishi had called for a snappier snap election.

Jeremy Nicholas
Great Bardfield, Essex

SIR – The more I read and see of the election shenanigans, the more I am tempted to follow advice I was once given for just such circumstances, namely, "Stand up, stretch, take a walk, go to the airport, get on a plane, never return."

Tony Tudor
Southport, Lancashire

SIR – No chance of a coup before July 4, I suppose?

Bruce Ridge
Clevedon, North Somerset

SIR – I fear that the "None of the Above" Party may well challenge Reform on July 4.

Neil Bunyan
Flitwick, Bedfordshire

SIR – When confronted by the dreaded decision as to who to vote for I have ensured the family is suitably up to the task. Everyone has been equipped with a clothes peg which, at the appointed time, is carefully applied across the nose.

Having blocked all unpleasant smells, one then has time to view the odious candidate list and vote. Whilst this method can't stop all the pain and anguish, it will help mitigate some of the side effects.

Tony Ellis
High Wycombe, Buckinghamshire

SIR – Waking up on the morning of Friday July 5, the nation will soon get firsthand insight into how the character Sam Tyler felt in *Life on Mars*, the TV series in which he wakes up after a car crash to find that he has time-travelled back to the depressing and oppressive union-dominated society of the 1970s.

Dr David Slawson
Nairn

SIR – I believe that almost total annihilation of the Tories at the upcoming general election is a foregone conclusion but I try to remain philosophical. As each generation will have its own music and street culture, so must it experience firsthand the realities of a Labour government. We will all survive somehow.

Frank Dixon
Thatcham, Berkshire

SIR – At last some good news: *Paddington 3* is coming soon. Maybe we should all keep a marmalade sandwich in our handbags or under our hats to weather the incoming government.

Tricia Barnes
Beaconsfield, Buckinghamshire

SIR – In idle moments I've occasionally wondered about the end of the world. It never occurred to me it would be Friday July 5 2024. On the bright side, I at least know where my towel is.

Catherine Farrell
Gosport, Hampshire

SIR – On Thursday I voted for Joe Biden. The poor old chap clearly needs all the help he can get.

Paul Berry
Barnstaple, Devon

The results are in

SIR – Bugger.

Ruth Ingram
Ledbury, Herefordshire

SIR – I looked at a map of the UK today and it was coloured predominantly blue. Unfortunately it was the predicted rainfall chart.

Michael Knox
Beaconsfield, Buckinghamshire

SIR – When the general election results came I expected Ed Davey to celebrate by jumping into the Thames. Disappointing.

Dan Hartley
Solihull, West Midlands

SIR – Cheer up everyone! We are already two days closer to the next general election.

Sue Hamilton-Miller
Twickenham, Middlesex

SIR – How are all the left-wing comedians going to write their jokes for the next few years?

David Wilkinson
Lincoln

SIR – The morning after the general election count I woke to a tremendous rainstorm and cold grey skies.

An hour later I was struck by one of my nasty migraines followed shortly by a power cut, meaning no coffee or tea.

Am I being punished for placing my cross in the wrong box?

Peter Gardner
Hydestile, Surrey

SIR – Ah well, and as the dust settles, I mark the 17th general election since 1964 in which I have voted for a losing candidate and political party. I find that reassuring. Life goes on.

Andy Trask
Liphook, Hampshire

Viral marketing

SIR – My local library appears to be at the forefront of the debunking of fake news. Matt Hancock's book, *The Pandemic Diaries,* was originally neatly shelved in the fiction section.

Jean Scoones
Yeovil, Somerset

Covid farce

SIR – I read in your newspaper that the Covid Inquiry is to begin a tour of the UK next week but sadly my home city Plymouth is not included in the itinerary.

We are lucky to have here in the South West a nationally acclaimed venue in the form of the Theatre Royal and our own pantomime *Snow White and the Seven Dwarfs* – the "Fairest panto in the land".

I initially thought the Covid Inquiry would have been the perfect sequel until I realised that the cast wages of £200k per diem might be a bit of a stretch for the good Burghers of Plymouth.

Nigel Theyer
Plymouth, Devon

SIR – I watched some of the Covid Inquiry broadcast yesterday. I won't dwell on that.

Does Dominic Cummings own an iron? If so, has he misplaced the instructions for it?

Bob Massingham
Bicester, Oxfordshire

SIR – One wonders what foul-mouthed invective Dominic Cummings would direct at a colleague who appears to lack a two-year-old's ability to get dressed in the morning. Oh, wait a minute…

Sandra Jones
Old Cleeve, Somerset

SIR – I really must do something to control my tendency to use strong language.

The thought that I could in some way be associated with government ministers and senior civil servants might go some way to encouraging a radical change in my behaviour.

Vincent Hearne
Chinon, Indre-et-Loire, France

SIR – After reading about the Covid Inquiry, I have decided that if I ever bought a racehorse I would name it Hindsight, because hindsight is a wonderful thing.

Linda Northover
Sidbury, Devon

SIR – As we see daily the millions of public money being wasted as each interviewee tells their own story and attempts to make themselves the only truthsayer and to bad mouth their peers, would it be a cheaper alternative for them all to have a conker competition which could be resolved in an afternoon?

We could then turn to the important issue of preparation for any further epidemics.

Judith Barnes
St Ives, Cambridgeshire

SIR – The easiest method for cutting this ridiculous inquiry short would be to conduct it the same way as some major companies operate. All meetings are conducted with no chairs or coffee. Most discussions are completed within an hour or so.

Tony Ellison
Westcliff-on-Sea, Essex

SIR – I have been wondering when Larry the cat was going to be interviewed for the Covid Inquiry. I have a hunch he may bring some order to the proceedings.

Susan Tuck
Cromer, Norfolk

SIR – Speaking as a simple arts graduate, it seems to me that Sir Patrick Vallance ate his cake some time ago, but is now claiming that it was actually Boris Johnson who ate it.

Christopher Hanson
Cheadle Hulme, Cheshire

SIR – During the lockdown our favourite entertainment was the nightly "Witless and Unbalanced" Pinky and Perky show. It provided much-needed light relief.

Kevin Smith
Trull, Somerset

Low on energy

SIR – May I, through your columns, offer advice to your readers: should they ever have to choose between using a camping stove and cooking by candlelight or using OVO as an energy supplier, they should order the Calor gas and lay in some candles and matches. It will be easier.

Sheila Houldin
Chester

SIR – Having just received the invoice for my winter log delivery I can confirm the existence of money trees.

Claire McCombie
Woodbridge, Suffolk

SIR – We must assume that after the ban on future North Sea oil contracts, the next fuel crisis that hits the world will find us heating our homes and running our cars on Ed Miliband's hot air.

Philip Hall
Petersfield, Hampshire

SIR – Ed Miliband's achievements in giving the go-ahead for Britain's biggest solar farm on green land (despite the objections of officials) and in ordering an immediate ban on drilling in new North Sea oil fields must be worthy of a promotion. Can I suggest Minister with Special Responsibility for Outer Mongolia? I understand it can be quite pleasant there at this time of year.

Phillip Wade
Cheltenham, Gloucestershire

Zero tolerance

SIR – We now have a major power supplier using TV advertising to declare its mission to "help cut UK carbon emissions to zero".

As a living, breathing carbon emitter I am beginning to feel quite uncomfortable.

Richard Sutcliffe
Charing Heath, Kent

SIR – Judging by the weather, Ed Miliband's policy on reducing global warming is already having an effect. Please could we pause the policy during the school holidays.

Mike Crowe
Cullompton, Devon

SIR – I am more worried about the mental/geriatric leaders with their fingers on the nuclear buttons than I am about global warming. If we are all blown to bits what will be left to warm?

Anne Senneck
Mere, Wiltshire

SIR – The last truly green people I can recall were the reptilian humanoid Treens, Dan Dare's implacable opponents in the *Eagle* comic of the 1950s. They weren't very helpful either.

Chris Spurrier
Hook, Hampshire

SIR – The ancient Mayans of Central America were experiencing climate change. They practised human sacrifice to try to stop it. Net Zero has not got that far…yet.

David Roche
London W2

SIR – In Cornwall we have a village trial of a green boiler fuel made with cooking fat. Today a Virgin flight has crossed the Atlantic using similar fuel.

Should we be eating more deep-fried food?

James Goad
Bodmin, Cornwall

They protest too much

SIR – I am considering tying one woke nutter to each of the eight hands on the four faces of Big Ben to protest against the fashionable tendency of vandalising statues, paintings and sculptures for various causes.

Robert Edwards
Hornchurch, Essex

SIR – I would like to compliment Mona Lisa on her composure after the soup attack by environmental protesters.

How many of us would still be smiling given the circumstances?

Andrew Shuttleworth
Saffron Walden, Essex

SIR – If the horses on carousels are replaced by cars, as proposed by Peta, the green brigade would object as they would glorify car ownership. Also the carousel is running on electricity which is wasteful.

I suggest that the horses are replaced by bicycles. The children riding them would apply the motive power.

This would then please everybody, except of course the people riding the carousel.

Allan Hook
Brighton, East Sussex

SIR – One wonders how far this Venn diagram approach to protest slogans will permeate.

May we expect "Just Stop Oil Gay Men Named Eric for a Free Palestine" any time soon?

Martin Hall
Welwyn Garden City, Hertfordshire

Sins of the fathers

SIR – Surely the time has come for the Church of England to atone for the Reformation.

Colin P. Young
Over Stratton, Somerset

SIR – Having researched my family history I find my lineage goes back to the Huguenots. How much has the French Catholic Church set aside for me?

Terry J. Gamble
Farnham Royal, Buckinghamshire

Sturgeon's new-found independence

SIR – Finally some good news from the SNP in Scotland. The former first minister Nicola Sturgeon has passed her driving test. Hopefully she will now be able to drive off into the distant sunset and will not be heard of again for a very long time.

Richard Allison
Edinburgh

The hating game

SIR – Watch out porridge eaters – the "Hate Monster" created by Police Scotland looks like an angry Weetabix.

John Simpson
Bracknell, Berkshire

SIR – I have been following your reports on the new hate crime legislation in Scotland and would like you to reassure me that there is no provision for extradition from Wales. I fear I have come to hate the SNP so much I might be guilty of some intangible crime.

Jeremy Douglas-Jones
Swansea

SIR – Disagreeable though it is, "hate" cannot plausibly be proscribed by law. I hate tattoos, boiled eggs and women's trousers with elasticated waistbands: does that criminalise me?

Michael Heaton
Warminster, Wiltshire

SIR – I wonder how many arrests will be made at this weekend's football match between Rangers and Celtic under Scotland's hate crime law. Anything under 48,000 would surely be deemed an abject failure.

Keith Snape
Fleetwood, Lancashire

SIR – The best definition of hate must be that expressed by Zsa Zsa Gabor:

"I never hated a man enough to give him his diamonds back".

Dennis Forbes Grattan
Aberdeen

SIR – Would the Westminster Government please provide the Scottish Government with free copies of the film *Barbie*?

With such a convincing argument in the movie for the rights of women and how we should all get along together, it can save thousands of hours of police and court time, and make human disagreements possible again in Scotland.

Keith Punshon
Thirsk, North Yorkshire

SIR – An unforeseen advantage of the Scottish and Welsh devolved assemblies is that they can be used to develop and test unwise policies, so that the rest of us don't have to.

James Masters
Bucknell, Shropshire

Fending for Yousaf

SIR – Humza Yousaf's resignation speech showed that he is a good family man.

Perhaps that is why he failed to realise that his approach to the Greens was the political equivalent of telling your wife you want a divorce, and then saying that you expect her to continue to have sex with you.

Gordon Pugh
Claygate, Surrey

Sorry, we're full

SIR – Before commenting on Britain's immigration policy, Archbishop Justin Welby would do well to remember that when Joseph and Mary went to the inn and were told there was no room, they did not say "we don't care, we are coming in anyway".

Larry Fisher
Redgrave, Suffolk

SIR – This morning I saw two magpies fighting over a scrap of roadkill on a busy A road. It reminded me of the Conservative MPs arguing over amendments to the Rwanda Bill while the two 18-wheelers that represent the Supreme Court's judgement on the law and the electorate's judgement on their competence bear down on them.

Richard Duncan
Guildford, Surrey

SIR – The Republic of Ireland is experiencing the issue that the UK faces with illegal immigration and is yet to come up with its own version of a Rwanda plan. However, the Republic is blessed with many offshore locations where immigrants could be sent.

I believe Craggy Island could do with a boost to its economy and population.

James Koltunicki
Belvedere, Kent

SIR – If we can't send illegal immigrants to Rwanda, could we at least send Gary Lineker there?

Jolyon Cox
Witney, Oxfordshire

SIR – The Home Secretary Yvette Cooper claims that Labour will stop small boats from illegally transporting migrants to the UK – presumably, one imagines, by replacing them with large boats.

Ron Freedman
Toronto, Canada

SIR – Is it quicker to get into the UK by inflatable dinghy or through an e-gate?

Simon Taylor
Poringland, Norfolk

Stray marbles

SIR – Could it be that the reluctance to return the Elgin Marbles is linked to the rising cost of postage?

Barrie Taylor
Highcliffe, Dorset

SIR – I am heartily sick to death of stories about returning items such as the Elgin Marbles to their original homes.

I have some underpants that were made in China and wondered where I could send them back to.

Tim Rann
Mirfield, West Yorkshire

SIR – Surely the only civilised way to settle the Elgin matter is with a game of marbles.

Philip Dennett
Burgess Hill, West Sussex

Going postal

SIR – Watching the latest incarnation of Postman Pat with my grandson today, I note that Mrs Goggins, the postmistress, no longer features. Does anyone know how many years she got?

Nick Pope
Woodcote, South Oxfordshire

SIR – Definition of "to commit a Horizon": to double down on a falsehood.

David Dunbar
Broadway, Gloucestershire

SIR – Hopefully Paula Vennells, the former chief executive of the Post Office, will use a courier service to ensure her CBE is returned safely.

Max Scott
Ipswich, Suffolk

SIR – Give Paula Vennells' CBE to Alan Bates. At least he deserves it.

Nick Kester
Wattisfield, Suffolk

SIR – Having watched the ITV drama about the Post Office scandal, I can understand why Paula Vennells would seem to be a perfect fit for senior management in the NHS.

Jeremy Collis
London SW19

SIR – I wonder if ITV or the BBC might consider creating a TV drama about problems with the NHS. They would be resolved overnight.

Bryan Thring
Long Crendon, Buckinghamshire

SIR – Has the time come to rename the colour "post office red"? Perhaps *fire engine red* would be less contentious.

Dr Roger Stevens
Yelverton, Devon

SIR – I have recently become aware of a steady thumping noise, which puzzled me somewhat until I realised that it was the noise of so many of our MPs jumping on the bandwagon of the Post Office scandal.

Ron Alder
Ipswich, Suffolk

Remember this

SIR – I appreciate the NHS is rather stretched at the moment but, while watching the Post Office Horizon Inquiry, I wonder if they are ready for a new epidemic; that of Post Office Amnesia Disorder.

It is alarming to watch so many sufferers giving evidence and I hope that a treatment will soon be available.

Lynne Walley
Etwall, Derbyshire

SIR – News that Post Office scandal victims may have to wait until 2026 for the Crown Prosecution Service to bring charges might present too big a challenge for Paula Vennells' memory.

Having watched and listened attentively to her three days of evidence at the Post Office Inquiry I fear that in another two years she will not be able to recall anything.

Peter Corrigan
Knutsford, Cheshire

SIR – Watching Paula Vennells giving evidence to the Post Office Inquiry, it was difficult to work out whether she would be given a prison sentence or an Oscar nomination.

Paul Morley
Skipton, North Yorkshire

SIR – Alan Bates did not follow the proper procedure for a knighthood. A big donation to the Tory Party is customary.

Derek McMillan
Durrington, West Sussex

Soldiers to the wheel

SIR – The Defence Secretary says he is sending 20,000 troops to a major defence exercise. How many of these are live personnel and how many are cardboard cutouts?

Colin Cummings
Yelvertoft, Northamptonshire

SIR – Can the Secretary of State and the members of the Army Board really afford to waste their dwindling reserves of ammunition by continuing to shoot themselves in the foot?

Charles Edward-Collins
Bodmin, Cornwall

SIR – I note the article in *The Daily Telegraph* on the MoD and the comments of think tanks.

They are probably the largest type of tank we have left.

Jonathan Batt
Castle Cary, Somerset

SIR – It was good to see a picture of the aircraft carrier HMS *Prince of Wales* in the *Telegraph*. It looks so neat and tidy and uncluttered. Unlike those US carriers that seem to have their decks covered with lots of those things called aeroplanes.

Edwin Fisher
Brentwood, Essex

SIR – I have just seen a beautiful model aircraft carrier, complete with jets, made from Lego: it is three feet long.
Should I send it to the MoD to help out?

Gill Noakes
Crowborough, East Sussex

SIR – Any elderly person will have sympathy with the Trident missile flop.

Archie Douglas
Whitton, Middlesex

New model army

SIR – General Sir Patrick Sanders wants people to be prepared to be called up in the event of war.
Good luck with that one, General: they'll probably want to work from home.

Malcolm Wood
Mold, Flintshire

SIR – If we are to recruit a citizen army, please don't give the job to Capita. The war will be over before they've arranged the first medical.

Ron Powell
Barry, Glamorgan

SIR – I read with interest Penny Mordaunt's call for a UK "Iron Dome" but wonder as to the cost and actual likelihood of a successful outcome.

I suspect we would end up with a partially completed "Tupperware Colander" constructed by the Chinese or the French on our behalf.

Ian Craig
Strathaven, Lanarkshire

SIR – Penny Mordaunt won't get the Iron Dome she has rightly called for. But worry not: any hostile nation that attempts to invade will be met by a veritable fire storm of inclusiveness, correct pronouns, hugs, focus groups and, of course, beards.

Malcolm Allen
Berkhamsted, Hertfordshire

Spoiling for a fight

SIR – I got quite excited when it was reported that Rishi Sunak was going to introduce conscription.

I was taught to fly with Leeds University Air Squadron between 1957 and 1960; the squadron was part of the RAF Volunteer Reserve. When I left in 1960 I think I was told that I would remain on the reserve forever.

Just to give Mr Sunak some encouragement, I am absolutely willing to be called back to fly my Chipmunk on active service for my country as soon as he likes, although I may have to be helped to climb the wing and get into the cockpit. Just tell me where and when.

Joseph Piercy
Peterborough, Cambridgeshire

SIR – I have always been a great fan of *Dad's Army*.
I never thought I'd be in it.

Alan Mottram (aged 75)
Tiverton, Cheshire

SIR – May I offer a helpful suggestion to those opposed to conscription? I strongly advise them to learn to speak Russian, because they will surely need it.

David Miller
Newton Abbot, Devon

SIR – I note that non-swimmers may now be recruited for the Royal Navy.
This would be a worry if any of them were ever asked to go to sea.

Phil Saunders
Bungay, Suffolk

SIR – Why all the fuss about non-swimming naval recruits?
You don't have to be able to fly to join the RAF.

Rupert Godfrey
Heytesbury, Wiltshire

SIR – You can tell it's the start of an election year. If in doubt, invade somewhere or bomb somebody.

Graham Low
Threapwood, Cheshire

The thinning blue line

SIR – News that Leicestershire is re-introducing blue lights outside police stations gives little cause for comfort to me in Hampshire. We don't appear to have any police stations left. I suppose that would, at least, minimise the expenditure on light fittings.

Rupert Tickner
Bordon, Hampshire

SIR – Why do we need police and crime commissioners?
I am of the opinion that we have more than enough crime without paying someone to commission more.

Colin Drummond
Falmouth, Cornwall

SIR – If Richmond and Bedford councils classify public urinating as a littering offence, watch out dog walkers.

Rob Dorrell
Bath, Somerset

SIR – If I self-identify as a dog will it enable me to urinate in the countryside without incurring a fine?

Richard Cowdell
Melton Mowbray, Leicestershire

SIR – The United Kingdom is no longer a nation of shopkeepers – it's a nation of shoplifters.

Christopher Hand
Bungay, Suffolk

SIR – Following the news that a Ferrari stolen 28 years ago has been recovered, can I hope that my Ford Fiesta stolen recently from Loughton might eventually turn up?

Sadly, if it does, I will probably be too old to drive.

Anne Saunders
Brampton, Cambridgeshire

SIR – With venison now on the prison menu, how on earth does one get banged up these days?

Alan Sabatini
Bournemouth, Dorset

SIR – *Misgendering a person*
Leaves you open to arrest,
Advocating jihad
Slips past the litmus test,
What's happened to our common sense?
Have we fallen from the tree
When a misplaced word is dangerous
And murder fancy free?

Angela Lanyon
Worcester

Clubs for the boys

SIR – For the life of me I cannot understand the furore over women being allowed to join a man's club.

The highlight of my week is Monday bridge night when I have the TV room and remote control to myself; I enjoy regular holidays with female friends. I'm very happily married but *vive la difference*!

Eve Wilson
Hill Head, Hampshire

SIR – There is a simple solution to the Garrick's inclusion and diversity dilemma. The members must all identify as male while on the premises, irrespective of biology or attire. Problem solved.

Deborah Tompkinson
Maidenhead, Berkshire

Stop the world, I want to get off

SIR – While I was driving the car recently, with young grandchildren in the rear, and discussing, with a front-seat, adult, passenger, the country's current journey "to Hell in a handcart", one of the grandchildren piped up: "Are we nearly there yet?"

Does anyone know the answer?

Dr Kevin M. O'Sullivan
Plymouth, Devon

SIR – In my humble opinion, what Trafalgar Square is crying out for is something that symbolises the times in which we live.

I propose a 3D representation of the figure in Edvard Munch's painting *The Scream*.

Truly, the plinth of wails.

Guy Bargery
Edinburgh

SIR – While travelling in Ireland I came upon the following poster:

"HAS ANYBODY TRIED UNPLUGGING THE COUNTRY AND PLUGGING IT BACK IN AGAIN?"

It applies to the UK as much as it does to Ireland.

Declan Salter
Chenies, Buckinghamshire

SIR – For four decades, if I was in London on a Sunday I would go to Speakers Corner. There was always a man there carrying a placard saying, "It's Going to Get Worse". I understand he died in early 2021. I was a Doubting Thomas, but it turns out that he was right.

Jonathan Yardley
Wolverhampton

SIR – With the banning of nitrous oxide now no one will have anything to laugh about in modern Britain.

John Kennedy
Hornchurch, Essex

HOME THOUGHTS ON ABROAD

Entente cordiale

SIR – I would have thought Emmanuel Macron was delighted to meet Sir Keir Starmer, if for no other reason than that it was an opportunity to be photographed with a political leader who was not in fact taller than him.

W. McLellan
Ashby Magna, Leicestershire

SIR – Starmer meets Macron; never trust a man who shakes hands with one hand while keeping the other firmly in his trouser pocket.

Ralph Stephenson
Stockbridge, Hampshire

Biden's time

SIR – Introducing a news bulletin from Israel, the excellent Lyse Doucet, resplendent in flak jacket and helmet, warned us, in obligatory BBC fashion, that we might find the following footage disturbing. She wasn't wrong. We were shown President Biden – descending, somewhat gingerly, the vertiginous steps of Air Force One. The idea that this gentleman is, de facto, the commander-in-chief of the free world disturbed me no end. President Trump, by contrast, would have been reassurance personified.

William Smith
Via email

SIR – I'd like to see anyone who thinks Biden is fit to run America give him the keys to their car and let him drive them around Washington DC for an hour.

Paul Gaynor
Windermere, Cumbria

SIR – I am really looking forward to the presidential campaign debates between Donald Trump and Joe Biden.

They will be comedy gold.

Joseph Chismon
Hitchin, Hertfordshire

SIR – Donald Trump has said that he was willing to undergo a test for performance-enhancing drugs before the debate.

He can save time as there is absolutely no evidence of enhanced performance and if he were taking such drugs he should ask for a refund.

Dennis Fitzgerald
Melbourne, Australia

SIR – The US presidential election: a choice between the quiff and the dead?

Toby Roberts
Cheltenham, Gloucestershire

SIR – Joe Biden's confusion saw him name his vice-president as Trump and the head of state in Ukraine as President Putin. Perhaps there's hope yet if he can be convinced that he's Michelle Obama.

Cameron Morice
Reading, Berkshire

Trump on trial

SIR – Poor Donald Trump, nodding off during the court proceedings against him. It's his age, you know. Doesn't matter so long as he's not in charge of anything important.

Alyson Persson
Henfield, West Sussex

SIR – Having listened to Mr Trump's statement following the court's verdict, I think there should be a further charge of murder: of the English language.

Innocence is a binary status, and cannot be qualified, as in "very innocent". Of course one must acknowledge that Mr Trump is very unique among past holders of the American presidency.

Jeremy Burton
Wokingham, Berkshire

SIR – Do Donald Trump and Geert Wilders share a barber?

Jim Jackson
Warlingham, Surrey

Shots fired

SIR – Donald Trump's reaction to the attempted assassination reminded me of the time when Ronald Reagan was shot. As the surgeons were preparing him for surgery he said: "'I hope you guys are all Republicans".

Sandra Lewin
Gerrards Cross, Buckinghamshire

SIR – It is a good thing that they do not have penalty shoot-outs in the US.

Chris Rome
Thruxton, Hampshire

SIR – It could have been much worse. Thank goodness President Biden mistakenly only called the ballot box the battle box, and not the bullet box.

Kevin Cottrell
Grosmont, Monmouthshire

Age before beauty

SIR – Given her impressive CV and obvious capabilities, could Americans not vote in the newly crowned Miss America as president?

Ella Douglas
Clevedon, Somerset

SIR – Two things make me smile each morning: Matt's cartoons and waking up to read about Joe Biden's latest overnight gaffe. I will miss the latter but will continue to take comfort in the former.

Phil Angell
Helston, Cornwall

SIR – Perhaps when Kamala Harris has rescued the Democrats she could call in and rescue *Strictly*.

Dr P.E. Pears
Coleshill, Warwickshire

From Russia with blood

SIR – The American commentator Tucker Carlson is absolutely correct when he states that Vladimir Putin doesn't threaten people with the sack when they disagree with him. He just arranges to have them killed.

Judith Rixon
Bourne, Lincolnshire

SIR – Putin says his "democracy" is transparent. Indeed it is. Entirely transparent. We can see right through it.

Susan Ellis
Midgham, Berkshire

SIR – "Stalin" was an adopted name, meaning Man of Steel.

Maybe Putin is Man of Putty.

Adam Massingham
Ashford, Kent

SIR – The Red Sea shipping disruption threatening tea shortages may be the last straw for this Government. The nation will grind to a halt. Send in the troops.

Kirsty Blunt
Sedgeford, Norfolk

SIR – Once again Vladimir Putin is threatening the West with nuclear weapons in case of further intervention in his "special military operation" against Ukraine. It is of course well known that Putin is a man of small stature and is about the same height as the originator of the term "Napoleon Complex" at 5 feet 7 inches. It is also well known that aggressors in the world are typically male and often shorter than average. Joseph Stalin was 5 feet 6 inches, Kaiser Wilhelm II about the same. Most female leaders involved in wars were on the defensive side, for example Margaret Thatcher responding to the invasion of the Falkland Islands.

While there are some aggressors who do not fit this pattern (General Galtieri for example standing at 6 feet 2 inches and Saddam Hussein being almost as tall), there does seem to be a connection between lack of stature and the desire to invade your neighbours. Perhaps what the world needs to do is restrict leadership of a country to females and males above a certain height – say 6 feet. While this would have denied us one of our finest Prime Ministers, Winston Churchill (5 feet 7 inches), he would not have been required to save the free world as Adolf Hitler (5 feet 9 inches) would have been prevented from becoming Führer and starting the Second World War.

Phil Mobbs (6 feet 2 inches)
Kendal, Cumbria

Nominative king

SIR – I see the new king of Denmark is Frederik X. Was he previously Frederik Twitter?

James Masters
Bucknell, Shropshire

Order, order

SIR – On a plane to Paris, my husband asked for "une biere". Imagine his surprise when, instead of the expected cold beer, he was handed a small teddy bear dressed in the livery of a pilot, complete with helmet and goggles.

Lindsay Marsh
Tiverton, Devon

SIR – On holiday with friends in Holland we were puzzled by a menu description and asked the waitress what type of meat it involved.

After some lengthy thought she announced with glee: "You know... Bambi". We decided to go veggie. Walt Disney has a lot to answer for.

P. Russell-Grant
West Mersea, Essex

SIR – We were in a pub in the Yorkshire Dales, where a young Italian lady was serving behind the bar. A hiker bounced in and said jovially, "Super day", to which she replied, "Minestrone". He very politely ordered it.

Jackie Hooley
Chandler's Ford, Hampshire

SIR – My wife and I had the *plat du jour* at a very nice French restaurant we came across some years ago.

My wife did not want the dessert so I attempted to change it for cheese. To this day I still think I got the French right, but it would appear from the laughter that I wanted to swap my wife for the cheese.

I am still married to a nice bit of camembert.

Robert Hurlow
Marnhull, Dorset

Back down to earth

SIR – On a recent Ryanair flight from Málaga I caught Covid.

Readers will be surprised that no extra charge was applied.

Alan Heap
Winchester, Hampshire

SIR – My husband and I arrived in Australia in 1968 on the day that England won the cricket at the Oval. The surly driver of the hotel minibus greeted us with: "Welcome to Australia, but if any of you Poms mentions the cricket you'll be thrown off my bus".

Barbara Dixon
Mansfield, Nottinghamshire

TRAVEL IN BRITAIN

Going nowhere fast

SIR – HS2 should be scrapped immediately and the funds diverted to providing a *Star Trek* type of "Beam Me Up" transportation.

This is likely to be completed considerably earlier and at a lesser cost than HS2.

Tony Parrack
London SW20

SIR – The second leg of HS2 is now to be shelved, which thankfully means we will no longer be subjected to the continual mispronunciation of the letter *H* by a greater part of the media.

M. Bransgrove
West Wittering, West Sussex

SIR – I can't see why there is a commotion about the scrapping of HS2. Very few trains seem to run nowadays at any rate.

Robin Nonhebel
Swanage, Dorset

A religious platform

SIR – I see that Network Rail has marked the month of Ramadan by displaying an Islamic message on the departure board at King's Cross Station.

Wish me luck as I travel to Riyadh, Saudi Arabia to hang up lights in a public area wishing everybody Happy Easter.

Graham White
Huntingdon

SIR – Given King's Cross Station thinks its sign boards are suitable to host religious messages (for Ramadan, if not for Lent), on Sunday I might return the favour and instead of preaching read out the number of delayed and cancelled train journeys from London's stations.

Rev David Ackerman
London W10

Along for the ride

SIR – Yesterday (October 30) I drove past a motorcyclist with an adult-size, grinning skeleton on his pillion seat. Said passenger was not wearing a helmet.

Was that a traffic offence?

Gordon Ratcliffe
Sherborne, Dorset

SIR – I have just seen a car, driven by a man with a phone held to his ear.

With the other hand he was picking his nose.

Advanced driving?

Ian Kerr
Coventry, Warwickshire

SIR – I was wryly amused by the sign seen today on the back of a Welsh Water tanker lorry. It said "non hazardous product". These days we obviously need that assurance.

Peter Roberts
Crickhowell, Brecknockshire

Driven to distraction

SIR – The paper reports a problem with Google's sat-nav app that has sent a number of unsuspecting drivers down a set of steps in Edinburgh.

To avoid similar problems when I'm driving, sometimes I watch where I'm going.

David Vincent
Hawkhurst, Kent

SIR – On the front page of the Business section you report that driverless cars could be on the road within four years. On a subsequent page it is reported that driverless cars are "going rogue" in San Francisco. In the meanwhile, I think that I will feel very much safer in my fifteen-year-old Volvo.

Ted Shorter
Tonbridge, Kent

SIR – If bikes with an electric motor are taxed and insured differently to motorbikes, might I register my electric car as a skateboard?

Brent Osborn-Smith
London SW1

SIR – My recollection of buying my first car brings on residual discomfort.

One showroom salesman's best pitch was: "The Ford Fiesta. That's a good woman's car."

"I am not a good woman", I barked as I stalked out, leaving him slack-jawed and open-mouthed.

Unfortunately, I bought a British Leyland disaster, a Mini Metro. I was soon ruder about them than I was to the hapless Fiesta salesman.

Anne Jappie
Cheltenham, Gloucestershire

SIR – My husband is on his second Porsche, another beautiful Boxster, with its sleek and classy lines.

As he is now 75, and I am 72, I have made a rule – no groaning as you lower yourself in and out of the seats.

Claire Moore
Melton Mowbray, Leicestershire

SIR – I was interested to read your article about Chinese cars as we have unknowingly hired one while in New Zealand. The steering is almost literally taken out of our hands, warning lights and hooters assail us for no apparent reason, and we are being watched, hopefully just for signs of fatigue. Nevertheless, we have decided not to talk politics when driving.

Wing Commander Roger Lindley (retd)
Tetbury, Gloucestershire

SIR – Twenty years ago I was showing my four-year-old daughter the various features of our new car. She thought for a moment and then asked: "Daddy, where's that thing that goes beep when somebody's a f—--g idiot?"

Paul Merrick
Richmond, Surrey

Sign language

SIR – While on a tour of St Lucia many years ago we saw a large sign painted on a rock face on a bend in the road. It was an advertisement for a funeral company, with a coffin and a caption which read "Drive carefully – we have your size!"

Susan Fleck
Cheltenham, Gloucestershire

SIR – A sign warning "Cats Eyes Removed" was placed where roadworks had taken place. Someone had an official-looking sign made and placed next to it. It read "Mice Very Happy".

Bill Ashton
Stockport, Cheshire

SIR – I'm still looking for the heavy plant crossing.

Jane Sequeira
Lytchett Minster, Dorset

There may be trouble ahead

SIR – On a recent trip to Antigua the young local guide on our coach was explaining the education system on the island and said "Even our driver is a PhD." We were very impressed – even more so when he quickly told us it stood for Pot Hole Detector.

Having had a very smooth journey we all felt there could be a lot of work for him in the UK.

Penny Wright
Westcliff on Sea, Essex

SIR – Today I discovered the best road in Devon. It is a stretch between Totnes and Newton Abbot signed "temporary road surface", where the upper layer of the tarmac seems to have been scraped off. Marvellous. Not a pothole in sight.

Jenny Arnold
Kingsbridge, Devon

SIR – We have renamed our road The Avenue of the Volcanoes after the range in Ecuador. with individual names for the largest. Cotopaxi is outside my gate.

Peter Colman
Rugeley, Staffordshire

SIR – While trudging head down in the rain on a Newcastle street, it occurred to me if there is one thing that appears impervious to weather and traffic, it is chewing gum. Perhaps that is what we should be mending potholes with.

Valerie O'Neill
(Currently visiting the UK)
East Perth, Australia

SIR – Surely the disgraceful state of our roads means that sleeping policemen are no longer necessary.

Carey Waite
Melksham, Wiltshire

SIR – The last time I can remember seeing a pothole repaired with any promptness was about a decade ago. A local Michelangelo had painted the defining image of masculinity around it (in rather lurid colours).

Tom Stubbs
Surbiton, Surrey

Out with the bang

SIR – I was sorry to read that Edinburgh Castle's One O'Clock Gun may become a thing of the past. While I was serving in the RN and my ship was visiting Rosyth one of my favourite pranks was to go to the Edinburgh tourist information office and enquire in a broad American accent: "What time do they fire the One O'Clock Gun?"

Simon Palmer
Portland, Dorset

SIR – How long will it be before the Scottish government determines that the Edinburgh Castle One O'Clock Gun is to be replaced by the District Gunner standing on the ramparts and shouting: "Hey you, Jimmie" at the top of his voice?

An awful lot of money would be saved and I am absolutely certain that tourists would appreciate the spectacle far more than real gunfire.

Colonel Philip Barry (retd)
Dover, Kent

East, west, home's best

SIR – While some may claim to be the world's top traveller, there is always a candidate for least travelled.

A former colleague recounted that her mother, Swansea-born and immensely proud of her roots, would assure people unfamiliar with the area that Swansea Bay was more beautiful than the Bay of Naples. She added, wonderingly, "I don't know how she claimed that, she'd never been further east than Newport."

Colin Drury
Dinas Powys, Vale of Glamorgan

SIR – Having recently returned from a hiking holiday in the beautiful Derbyshire Peak District I would like to thank those dog owners that provide a valuable service by providing markers for walkers unfamiliar with the terrain. All pedestrian routes are now easily navigated by following the trail of plastic bags of dog droppings that decorate dry stone walls, hedges, fences and footpaths, making orientation a walk in the park.

Patrick Gurr
Richmond, Middlesex

SIR – My nephew would like to know whether he can identify as a seagull so that he can go round stealing chips on the seafront in St Ives.

Linda Beskeen
Redruth, Cornwall

SIR – Overheard on a Porthcawl beach – Mother to a screaming child: "Enjoy yourself or I'll 'it you!"

Dr P. J. Law
Cwmbran, Monmouthshire

THAT'S ENTERTAINMENT

No laughing matter

SIR – I wish to formally complain about the coverage of allegations made against Russell Brand. The description of this man, promulgated by the mainstream media, has now been taken up by the *Daily Telegraph*. There is a definite push to describe him as a comedian.

Don McBurney
York

SIR – I'm sure Mr Brand is delighted that, as he pleads his innocence, he has been supported by Andrew Tate and Elon Musk.

All he needs now is support from Donald Trump and Vladimir Putin and his reputation is watertight.

Patrick Fuller
Upper Farringdon, Hampshire

This is our BBC

SIR – The BBC is going to "assess if there is any evidence of groupthink". I wonder if everyone will conclude that there isn't.

Henry Maj
Armitage, Staffordshire

SIR – Petronella Wyatt criticises cultural appropriation in the new BBC series of *Wolf Hall: The Mirror and the Light*. If it is anything like the previous series, it will be too dark to detect the colour of the actors' skin and also pretty much inaudible.

Fiona Wild
Cheltenham, Gloucestershire

SIR – A more apt title for *Strictly Come Dancing* is *Carry On Screaming.*

Michael Knight
Taunton, Somerset

SIR – *The Great British Sewing Bee* is back, fast down the straights, tricky through the corners and ending in the occasional car crash – not unlike *Top Gear,* another of my favourites.

Best of all though: no trigger warnings!

Andrew Gaisford
Tockenham, Wiltshire

Her indoors

SIR – Monty Don's wife is never seen or heard on *Gardeners' World*, rather like the wife of Lieutenant Columbo, the LAPD detective.

However, just to show that Mrs Don is not a fictitious character, I would suggest that she plays an occasional part in her husband's programme. Towards the end, when Monty is giving us our jobs for the weekend, a female voice should be heard to call out: "Monty, how much longer are you going to be in that bloody garden? Your tea's going cold!"

David S. Ainsworth
Manchester

Politics live

SIR – I generally watch television using subtitles. Sometimes they are a joy. I have just seen Chris Mason, interviewing Liz Truss, call her "You slack-jawed sanswer!".(Later corrected to "you sacked your own chancellor").It makes politics seem very interesting.

Liz Wheeldon
Seaton, Devon

SIR – There are a number of recent articles along the lines of "Who won *The Traitors*?". Really, I am much more interested in real traitors, backstabbing, cheating and people out of their depth, so I occasionally tune into televised Parliament – and yes, the Australian Parliament is just as bad as the British stuff.

Why watch reality TV when there is much better entertainment available in the real world, and there are no ads?

Dennis Fitzgerald
Melbourne, Australia

SIR – Why did the ITV party leaders' debate take place in the Tardis? And why didn't it take off with the leaders within?

Jenny Arnold
Kingsbridge, Devon

SIR – The Labour Party does not need political party broadcasts – it has the BBC News.

Anthony Skipper
Norwich, Norfolk

SIR – My husband has just kindly given me a new pair of ear defenders. Sorry Angela Rayner, but he knows my limits – so we can now watch the news together.

Charlotte MacKay
Shaftesbury, Dorset

SIR – As I never survive to the end of any news bulletins I am writing to suggest that the weather forecast should come at the beginning.

C M Watkins
Brentwood, Essex

On the airwaves

SIR – Why do Classic FM presenters sound as if they are broadcasting to the under-threes and the over-90s?

Trevor Pratt (aged 56)
Leatherhead, Surrey

SIR – Radio 4 is to end the very pleasant one-minute broadcast of "Tweet of the day" which starts my morning at one minute to six each day.

May I suggest as a replacement programme a one-minute piece taken from *Yesterday in Parliament* entitled "Twit of the day".

The programme could run for years.

Raymond Kite
Keston, Kent

SIR – The reason that the BBC *Today* programme is losing listeners is that it is so yesterday.

Barrington Mumford
Stone Allerton, Somerset

Drama is the best medicine

SIR – *Coronation Street* has a GP who is accessed within minutes, does house calls and seems to work around the clock. I can only assume that the script writers all use private medical services or rely on very long memories.

Jane Moth
Stone, Staffordshire

SIR – Watching a not-so-old episode of *Midsomer Murders*, I noted that much suspicion was aroused by the fact that an ambulance had taken nearly 90 minutes to respond to a call.

Those were the days!

Cliff Brooker
Hastings, East Sussex

Man of a certain age

SIR – John Cleese claims Basil Fawlty would be bewildered by today's England. Indeed, one can picture Basil, eyes bulging at a vegan brunch, wrestling with a smartphone, and ranting at a contactless payment machine. Perhaps it's just as well that he's stuck in the 1970s. Modern life would be far too much for his frayed nerves; I fear it is mine.

David McCreadie
Hindhead, Surrey

Rise to the challenge

SIR – If Amol Rajan were to speak even faster perhaps there would be more questions we would be capable of answering.

Gilly Atkins
Pulborough, West Sussex

Ads insult to injury

SIR – If there is a Hell, if there's any justice in this universe it will be filled with the lyricists to all those badly metered TV adverts for Bold and Flash.

Mark Boyle
Johnstone, Renfrewshire

Bring the noise

SIR – Aristotle taught that music has the power to alter the character of the soul. Heaven only knows what he would have made of the UK's showing at Eurovision – unmelodious as well as lewd and tacky. One can only hope the event was beamed across the globe. Forget Border Force controls: the threat of exposure to such musical horrors could be the most effective deterrent of all. Olly Alexander, your country needs you!

Dr Catherine Moloney
Liverpool

SIR – Enjoyment of the highly entertaining but über-woke blingfest that is the Eurovision Song Contest would be enormously enhanced if the scoring took place first with the songs to follow. The results would be the same, but we wouldn't have to sit through the "songs" and barely coded messages from virtue-signalling performers.

Charles Foster
Chalfont St Peter, Buckinghamshire

SIR – Whatever your viewing habits, it is hard to stomach subsidising a jolly for 1,000 members of BBC staff at the Glastonbury Festival.

If it did the same for snooker I might be more sympathetic.

Maria McGee
Derry, Northern Ireland

SIR – As Glastonbury approaches, I have to inform you that –

I must go down to Worthy Farm
For sex and drugs and rock and roll
To dance around wearing just one welly
Before the years take their toll.

Yes, I must go down to Worthy Farm
To plant my tent in its muddy land
Before I'm old and rickety
Like the singer in the headline band.

Ken McAdam
London W13

SIR – We have a full complement of four daughters with PTSD: Post Taylor Swift Depression.

Sue McFadzean
Swansea

Given fair warning

SIR – I am watching the excellent film *The Zone of Interest* on Amazon Prime and noticed that the trigger warnings only advised the fact that the film contains alcohol use and smoking. I suppose that's fair enough as I can't imagine anything else a film concerning the commandant of Auschwitz might include that could be upsetting.

David Magasiner
Wisbech, Cambridgeshire

This great stage of fools

SIR – If the theatre director Jenny Sealey's logic – that able-bodied actors shouldn't play Richard III – is carried into other Shakespeare plays, then mentally stable actors shouldn't play King Lear or Hamlet.

Michael Bacon
Bordon, Hampshire

SIR – If able-bodied actors are deemed unsuitable to play the part of Richard III, who is eligible to play Banquo's ghost?

Jolyon Cox
Witney, Oxfordshire

SIR – I was once asked to play the Mad Hatter in a production of *Alice in Wonderland* by our local amateur group. I am now wondering whether the casting director was sending me a message.

Graham Fish
Hertford

SIR – The Soho Theatre in London has asked white patrons to "check their privilege at the door".

As I intend to join the patrons I shall demand a receipt, so that I may reclaim it on my way out.

George Kelly
Buckingham

SPORTING TRIUMPH AND DISASTER

The referee's a –

SIR – We must get rid of VAR; then we can go back to whinging about the referee again. Where's the joy in doubting VAR's parenthood?

Mark Rayner
Eastbourne, East Sussex

Pray and play

SIR – Surely with players Jesus and Gabriel in their side, Arsenal should win the Premiership Title this season.

Paul Simpson
Pyrford, Surrey

SIR – Nike is quoted as saying that the new interpretation of the Cross of St George on the England football shirt is intended to "unite and inspire".

Judging by much of the feedback, perhaps a more accurate description would be to "incite and backfire".

Stuart Harrington
Burnham-on-Sea, Somerset

SIR – I am really not sure why the England football team will be sporting a Chevrolet logo on their shirts.

Roger Westwell
Glossop, Derbyshire

SIR – I don't know about St George's Cross; I should think he's bloody livid.

Martin Wiley
Goffs Oak, Hertfordshire

SIR – I wonder how Nike would respond if the FA displayed their logo upside down on the England shirt – just as a playful little update, you understand.

Kenneth Hayden-Sadler
Teignmouth, Devon

England expects

SIR – I see on social media that plenty of Scottish separatists are now adopting an ABE (Anyone but England) approach to Euros 24. Presumably, that's because SNP (Scotland's not playing).

Martin Redfern
Melrose, Roxburghshire

SIR – After watching last night's game against Slovenia, I suggest that Nigel Farage should be appointed as England manager immediately. This should introduce some urgency and much-needed objectivity into our game in time for the knockout stages.

Ian Johnson
Chelford, Cheshire

SIR – It takes a special skill to be given the very expensive parts for a Rolls Royce team but to build a Trabant from them for the first three games.

Gareth Southgate needs retraining.

Keith Phair
Felixstowe, Suffolk

SIR – Are statistics available comparing the England team results when the manager was wearing a tie and waistcoat with his current attire? At this point in time surely anything is worth consideration.

Tony Webb
Buckhurst Hill, Essex

SIR – England are a waistcoat short of a fitting performance.

Andrew McGrath
Teddington, Middlesex

SIR – I have been sleeping rather poorly of late so am most grateful to Gareth Southgate and his team.

Peter Flood
Guildford, Surrey

SIR – At 85 it is customary to contemplate one's own passing. Also normal is to dwell upon the various scenarios. It is rare to think of dying of boredom. But if I have to watch any more England-v-Offshore Island Internationals I may have to put sheer ennui at the top of the list.

Frederick Forsyth
Beaconsfield, Buckinghamshire

SIR – We wanted football, not pinball.

NP Scott
Reigate, Surrey

SIR – I note that St Jude (Bellingham) is the patron saint of lost causes.

David Langridge
Lewes, East Sussex

SIR – Against all the odds, the England team have continually won their games and progressed despite one abysmal performance after another. The England team are led by a manager who appears as dull as ditch water and tacitly tin-eared.

Politics and football are very relatable right now.

Warren Stocks
Echt, Aberdeenshire

SIR – Groups of 22 men have been kicking a ball about. This has created so much fuss and bother, so much television time, so much newspaper coverage, so many shrieks of delight or horror, that I am back to a conclusion that I came to many years ago.

Football is a waste of grass.

Elizabeth Charlesworth
Loughborough, Leicestershire

Into penalty time

SIR – The Euros competition has now reached the knock-out stages. My grandson suggests that in the event of a draw after extra time the team with the most tattoos should win. This would save the agony of penalties.

John Tilsiter
Via email

SIR – I am always surprised that when taking a penalty kick the player does not suddenly stop his approach, look up at the sky as though he's spotted something amazing and point in astonishment, thus causing the goalie to look up likewise and leave a window of opportunity for a goal. My brother used to do this to me when he was after my sweets and it always worked.

Liz Wheeldon
Seaton, Devon

SIR – As I am on holiday in Scotland, I will be watching the Euros final in a crowded pub.

I have bought a Spanish shirt, as well as a chain to restrain me if I leap out of my seat if we score.

Phil Saunders
Bungay, Suffolk

SIR – We can do it lads. Think of The Spanish Armada!

Jacqueline Davies
Faversham, Kent

The pain continues

SIR – Labour promised change in the run-up to the election. Spain 2 England 1. Evidence of a disappointing broken promise so early in their tenure.

James Neal
Woodbridge, Suffolk

SIR – As the exculpatory discourse continues over yet another tournament failure by the England team, I wonder whether sports officials facing the nation's collective wrath have given any consideration to the question of whether climate change was a factor in the squad's hopeless performance. It is, after all, blamed for so many other adverse outcomes despite the complete absence of proof.

Kevin Duffy
Manchester

SIR – We have the ideal successors to Gareth Southgate: step forward Gary Lineker and Alan Shearer. They have all the answers already.

Garry Critchley
Liverpool

Lineker avoids a red card

SIR – I believe that XL Bully dogs will be muzzled in public in the future.

Could the same please be applied to Gary Lineker?

Martyn Collinson
Chichester, West Sussex

SIR – Gary Lineker says he tweets so that "I can look at myself in the mirror at night". One gets the impression that he looks in the mirror rather more often than that – and very much likes what he sees.

John Mounsey
Minchinhampton, Gloucestershire

SIR – Allison Pearson writes about her experiences of watching the Euros, including seeing Gary Lineker's shameless promotion of his Next range. I couldn't help but notice that even he cannot avoid the gradual change into Alan Partridge which besets nearly all men of a certain age.

Mark Robbins
Bruton, Somerset

SIR – Can any sports star be more passé than a "former legend"?

Gordon Brown
Grassington, North Yorkshire

The good, the bad and the rugby

SIR – When I was very young, my father decided to teach me how to skip in our farmhouse kitchen. The lesson ended abruptly, however, when my father's hair got tangled in a fly paper that was hanging from the ceiling. He could only be extricated by my mother wielding a pair of scissors.

The resulting mullet would not have looked out of place on today's international rugby field.

David Mitton
Skipton, North Yorkshire

SIR – I disagree with your esteemed rugby correspondent's call for the haka to be scrapped.

Rather, the England team's response should be a choreographed performance of a Morris dance, complete with sticks, bells and a grand flourish of flowery handkerchiefs.

Bob Clough-Parker
Chester

Littler joins the big league

SIR – I had always thought that the shape of a darts player was directly related to the time he had spent learning his trade in pubs. At 17, Luke Littler suggests there must be another reason.

Roger Foord
Chorleywood, Hertfordshire

SIR – Unless he lays off the junk food he is rumoured to enjoy, Luke Littler will never live up to the injunction of his own name.

Hugh Hetherington
Sandwich, Kent

Matchless style

SIR – I see that Wimbledon is retaining the line judge dress code – white trousers and blue shirt, with the gentlemen wearing ties while the ladies don't.

In today's new society one wonders what the tie-policy is for the other 70 genders.

Bill Soens
Ormskirk, Lancashire

SIR – Wimbledon again – and exciting new players to watch. Just love Mark Lajal's hair style, we have christened it "the corn sheaf".

Veronica Rickards
Ripon, North Yorkshire

SIR – I wanted to be a professional tennis player, but I couldn't manage all the fist-pumping.

Is it obligatory?

Vincent Hearne
Chinon, Indre-et-Loire, France

Hit parade

SIR – I am baffled as to why the England and Wales Cricket Board has not yet involved Snoop Dogg in the plans for The Hundred. Mr Dogg seems entirely suited to the competition. What's more, he will have just as much knowledge and love of the game of cricket as some of the names mentioned on your pages.

Graham Fish
Hertford

704 wickets and out

SIR – I am sure that all we cricket lovers can think of at least 704 reasons why the great Jimmy Anderson should receive a knighthood for services to sport.

Wonderful cricketer and an example to which all young players should aspire.

Kim Potter
Lambourn, Berkshire

For peat's sake

SIR – How many other countries can boast of holding a World Bog Snorkelling Championship? There is "Great" in Britain after all.

Lucinda Roberts
Crediton, Devon

En garde!

SIR – Were I ever to become a member of the Olympics Committee I would be looking at ways of making some of the sports a better experience for those watching. The first sport that needs an urgent revamp is fencing. Surely this should be staged in a mock-up of a mediaeval castle with extra points being earned for swinging across the great hall on a chandelier; sliding down a tapestry using a dagger; slicing through a row of candles and fighting backwards while going up a tight spiral staircase (glass walled like a squash court so the spectators can see it all).

Richard Sinnerton
Sunningdale, Berkshire

Opening gambit

SIR – What a joy to watch the athletes waving flags at the opening ceremony instead of mobile phones.

Alyson Warren
Henley-on-Thames, Oxfordshire

SIR – While I appreciate that the French make the best lovers in the world, having sat through four hours of egalitarian mediocrity before reaching a climax I am rather proud to be British.

Freddie Banks
Via email

SIR – As "taking offence" now seems to be the national sport of Britain and numerous other Western nations, when can we expect to see it in the Olympics?

Jeremy Dixon
Wilmslow, Cheshire

SIR – Before anyone starts, please can broadcasters and other media types note that there is no such verb as "to medal". You might win a medal or be awarded one, but to repeatedly hear that someone had "medalled" at the Olympics put quite enough unnecessary strain on my blood pressure last time around.

Thank you in advance.

Charles Smith-Jones
Landrake, Cornwall

LONG TO REIGN OVER US

Ginger whinger

SIR – Would someone be kind enough to send Prince Harry a large stock of lozenges? The poor boy's throat must surely be raw after all the interminable whining.

Geoff Millward
Sandside, Cumbria

SIR – Presumably Harry and Meghan are called H and Meg to distinguish them from the shopping destination of H&M.

Elizabeth Edmunds
Hassocks, West Sussex

SIR – An interesting photograph of the Duchess of Sussex wearing an anti-stress patch on her left arm while holding a mobile phone in her right hand. Is that not like carrying a diet book and a cream bun at the same time?

Mark Macauley
Heytesbury, Wiltshire

SIR – How splendid that Prince William wants the fighting to stop in the Middle East. We would all like the fighting to stop in the Royal Family.

Tom Harrison
Winslow, Buckinghamshire

One picture, a million words

SIR – The Princess of Wales is being castigated for making a few edits to a Mother's Day photograph.

When the late Queen was filmed having tea with Paddington Bear, in celebration of her Platinum Jubilee, I don't remember any complaints. In fact we all loved it.

Alexandra King
Ibthorpe, Hampshire

SIR – I suppose that, when you think about it, every painted portrait in Buckingham Palace has been "manipulated".

Matthew Darroch-Thompson
Bury St Edmunds, Suffolk

SIR – When I worked for a government agency the annual report contained a photo of the management board. One year it was decided to alter the photo to take out a bandage on the female director's knee. She objected and the bandage was reinstated.

Chris Yates
Peasedown St John, Somerset

SIR – We all know that body doubles for Kate and William and their children have been on the Palace payroll for years. It was obviously these who were photographed shopping in the local village store this week. And while we are at it, we also know that the King died two months before the Coronation, that Queen Camilla is training to be an astronaut, and that Lord Lucan was seen riding Shergar in Windsor Great Park last week.

Barrie McKay
Milton Abbas, Dorset

SIR – Back in the old days every village had an idiot but they were isolated. Now they can all talk to one another.

Rodney Francis
Brentwood, Essex

In public, in private

SIR – Among the reasons given for the disgraceful intrusion in the private health matters of the Princess of Wales, and, indeed, the King, is that "we pay for them and therefore have a right to know".

In which case, I look forward to perusing the health records of my local MP, school teachers and the binman.

Justice Hawkins
Great Torrington, Devon

SIR – You suggest that China and Russia are behind the stream of disinformation about the Princess of Wales in a bid to destabilise our nation. Why bother? I would say we've managed that on our own.

Kirsty Blunt
Sedgeford, Norfolk

Portrait of a king

SIR – The portrait of the King by Jonathan Yeo is to be highly recommended, and the facial likeness is remarkable, but why should His Majesty be portrayed floating in a bowl of tomato soup?

Clive Kaiser-Davies
East Grinstead, West Sussex

SIR – The new official portrait of the King does have one redeeming feature.

If the Just Stop Oil vandals target it with red paint, it will not show.

John Snook
Sheffield, South Yorkshire

SIR – I thought Animal Rising's "defacement" of the King's portrait rather improved it. As far as I am aware it did not damage the artwork and was easily removed. But it did the trick – it got them publicity.

Duncan Rayner
Sunningdale, Berkshire

Cream of the crop

SIR – You report that yesterday the King and Queen were lucky enough to attend a potato-growing competition on Jersey.

On occasion one feels for members of the Royal Family. How does one look interested during a potato-growing competition?

Tim Reid
Mayfield, East Sussex

SIR – Does the visit of the King and Queen to a certain Channel island make them Jersey Royals?

Sandra Hancock
Exeter, Devon

Pop princess

SIR – I know that it is no longer permissible to beat naughty children, but what on earth did the royal youngsters do that was so wrong to make Prince William take them to a Taylor Swift concert?

Clive Pilley
Westcliff-on-Sea, Essex

USE AND ABUSE OF LANGUAGE

News-speak

SIR – Why is it that weather forecast presenters say, "It's going to be raining out there?" Unless you have a leaking roof it's unlikely to be anywhere else.

Harriet Crocker
Bristol

SIR – I am surely not alone in wondering where exactly is "I luv man", frequently referred to in the BBC radio shipping forecast.

Roger Wilson
Charter Alley, Hampshire

SIR – On learning that *Springwatch*'s Gillian Burke thinks that African animals should be referred to, on British television, by their Swahili names, I cannot help but wonder if there is an easy-to-learn Swahili phrase meaning "virtue-signalling idiot".

Michael Oak
Stirling

SIR – In future I will not be "going forward".

Garth McGowen
Ely, Cambridgeshire

What it says on the packet

SIR – I am always curious about Tyrell's potato crisps which are "Cooked by hand".

How hot do the hands need to be?

Faith Scott
Farnham, Surrey

SIR – I am one of many who are partial to a portion of a well-known brand of luxury vanilla ice cream with a French-sounding name. Am I alone in being far from reassured by the labelling "Sustainable, Hand-picked".... and "Containing 93% less plastic"?

Gordon Ratcliffe
Chetnole, Dorset

SIR – Both my wife and I are partial to hot cross buns. However, despite their packaging, every single one we have ever bought has been cold.

Bob Ferris
Banstead, Surrey

SIR – I was presented with some estate agents' details which mentioned that the kitchen was blessed with a "free range cooker". Obviously, one which would move around the house at will.

Bryony Hill
Hurstpierpoint, West Sussex

SIR – As someone who has no canine companion I find the instruction that "dogs must be carried" at the top or bottom of an escalator somewhat limits my options.

Philip Dodd
Wooburn Moor, Buckinghamshire

Gender agenda

SIR – Let us hope God is a woman.

With Anneliese Dodds and Bridget Phillipson defining "women" we are going to need all the help we can get.

Sue Newth-Gibbs
Brentwood, Essex

SIR – I was surprised to read in the short article about a retiring stud dog that Trigger was referred to as "it". As the article was celebrating his, clearly male, accomplishments, I don't think there is any doubt about his biological sex. Neither do I think he'll be offended by the pronoun "he".

In fact, in my experience, biological males with a reputation of being a prolific stud are quite proud of their male status.

Tracey Wood
Midland, Michigan, United States

SIR – Gender obsession is gripping the country. I suggest when presented with a box marked "sex" everyone should say "yes".

Camilla Coats-Carr
Teddington, Middlesex

SIR – I share the irritation of Jonathan Agnew at the BBC's gender-neutral terminology.

What will happen to the cricketer who bowls a maiden over?

David Kilner
Corbridge, Northumberland

SIR – A subscriber to a book printed in Carmarthen in 1771, one Richard Bevan of Swansea, describes himself as a surgeon and a man-midwife.

Robert Pugh
Llandeilo, Carmarthenshire

SIR – Isn't "John" Lewis a bit too gender specific for comfort?

Dr John Doherty
Stratford-upon-Avon, Warwickshire

SIR – Your report on the recent murder trial held at Oxford Crown Court reveals that judges have been instructed to "respect" the gender identity of defendants and to allow them to choose the pronouns used to refer to them during the proceedings.

Should I ever find myself in court, I would not mind whether I was referred to using either the masculine or feminine form, but would quite like the idea of being addressed as "Your Majesty".

David Vincent
Cranbrook, Kent

SIR – Sir/madam/to whom it may (or may not) concern

In anticipation of mandatory preferred pronouns I have become an early adopter.

Howard Lewis-Nunn
(one/one's)
Via email

On overfamiliar terms

SIR – I notice that Lady Victoria Starmer is called "Vic" by her husband and others. I very much doubt they would dare call her "Tori" which is often used.

Angela Walters
Princes Risborough, Buckinghamshire

SIR – I now have an agreement with my wife that I will allow three "strikes" being addressed as *mate*, *buddy* or similar before I respond by addressing the offender as *blossom*, *pet*, *sweety pie* or any other form which comes to mind at the time.

Graham Jones
Tytherington, Cheshire

SIR – I am recovering from my recent bout of familiarity. I am 77 and live down a lane which the bin lorry can't access. So I haul our bins 150 yards up this lane every week.

Half-way up the lane this week, while struggling – obviously not manfully – with the heavy garden waste bin I was met by this glorious smiling young thing who made me think "I've still got it." She said, "Can I take the bin for you, sir?"

When I got home and I told my wife this sorry tale, she patted me on my (bald) head and said, "Yes, Pet."

Nick Nelson
Iwerne Minster, Dorset

SIR – Now aged 80, I have just returned from Cornwall, where younger ladies in two National Trust properties and a tollbooth at the Tamar Bridge crossing all called me "my lovely", with a smile. I'm not complaining – I'm not treated as well as this in Surrey.

Allen Chubb
Grayswood, Surrey

SIR – What I object to is being asked "Are you alright there?". A friend of mine deals with that by responding: "Not really, my piles are terrible today but thank you for asking".

Simon Bathurst Brown
Camberley, Surrey

Money talks

SIR – Lloyds Bank has issued an inclusive language guide for its staff. It stresses the danger of using words with strong negative associations. I suggest that they start by finding an alternative for *banker*.

Trevor Jones
Sidmouth, Devon

SIR – You reported that the dismissal of a banker was justified as he was dishonest in his expenses claim.

Using the word *expensing* should carry a similar sanction.

Jeremy Douglas-Jones
Swansea

SIR – I am lettering you after the surprise I got while porridging this morning. You article that a man has been sacked for "expensing his partner's lunch". Is this correct terming? I have been dictionarying and it seems it is not. Please don't let the language in your paper de-qualitise in this way.

Sue Thomas
Monmouth

Sorry to ask

SIR – Another unreserved apology. How do you make a reserved apology?

John Whitley
Leeds, West Yorkshire

SIR – Am I unique in finding things that are very unique superfluous?

John R. M. Prime
Havant, Hampshire

SIR – Why are the vast majority of majorities vast?

Brian Simpson
Dinas Powys, Vale of Glamorgan

SIR – Is there any product or service remaining which isn't "incredible"?

Andrew Blake
Marlborough, Wiltshire

SIR – Is the collective noun for a group of "uni" students *units*?

David Barlow
Cury, Cornwall

SIR – I've noticed that many people in the UK claim to be filling forms out. How does that differ from filling forms in, which is what I have always done?

Peter McPherson
Merriott, Somerset

SIR – I am so fed up with the grammatically questionable "fed up of".

Douglas Brett
Bideford, Devon

SIR – Can someone tell me when "back in the day" was?

Lynda Cox
Southampton

Stand and deliver

SIR – If politicians were forbidden from using the word "deliver" or any derivation, would they be unable to communicate with us? And would that be a bad thing?

Brian Lipman
East Barnet, Hertfordshire

SIR – Whatever would politicians do without the words: "We've been very clear"?

R. L. Smith
Bristol

SIR – Even my daughter tells me she is going to see Taylor Swift "fully costed, fully funded".

This one is true: by me.

Mike Forlan
Hayling Island, Hampshire

SIR – I made a vow that, every time I heard "fully costed, fully funded" in this campaign, I would have a gin and tonic.

Now feeling really pished/unwell. Hopefully better in the morning.

Alan Phizacklea
Marlborough, Wiltshire

Out of office

SIR – If former leading civil servants and diplomats feel that the full title of their department – the Foreign, Commonwealth and Development Office (FCDO) – is "anchored in the past", then a simple change is required.

We have a Home Office, so why not the Away Office?

David Dunn
Málaga, Spain

We don't need no education

SIR – I received an email from my son's secondary school: "Just to inform you that when your son/daughter returns to school Monday 3 July 2024 the stationary shop will have increased there prices.

"Attached to this email is the new price list going forward from June 2024."

He is sitting his English language GCSE this week. Should I be concerned?

Julie Trent
Via email

Effing and jeffing

SIR – In order to be consistent should we now expect the Haitch Brigade to mispronounce other letters of the alphabet as well? I look forward to hearing Feff, Lell, Memm and Rarr to mention just a few.

Brian Pike
Fareham, Hampshire

SIR – When we watch Wimbledon or any other tennis tournaments, we hear the following strange words from the commentators:

Se
Poin
Hi
Sho
Cour
Raque

I have found a way of translating these words into English – add a "t" to the end of the strange sound. Try it!

Ian Franklin
Totnes, Devon

SIR – An old friend once held a senior position with Cunard. When asked by new acquaintances what he did for a living, he would reply quickly: "I work f' Cunard". Unsure whether they had heard him correctly, many newcomers raised an eyebrow.

Bruce Denness
Niton, Isle of Wight

SIR – In the early 1970s I moved from London, back to the North, working as an engineer.

I looked after a large room, full of machines wrapping mini rolls, each operated by fine Northern ladies. If a problem occurred a loud Tannoy message would request "that engineer what speaks proper".

Alan France
Marlow, Buckinghamshire

A name to conjure with

SIR – Nearly 60 years ago when I started at Leeds University, I became friendly with a girl whose surname was Waugh. One day she told me that she would have loved a double-barrelled name. I responded: "What, like Waugh-and-Peace?" She never spoke to me after that.

Keith Haines
Belfast

SIR – If the Met Office is going to give storms names, can it please give them names everyone can pronounce.

George Brown
Manchester

SIR – Surely, one of the benefits of leaving the EU must be to name our own storms. As it is, they appear to be named by the Irish and Dutch Met Offices. The result is utterly unfamiliar names like Babet, Ciaran, and Debi. I must admit that I make up my own names, so that they are familiar, like Bert, Charlie and Dave. These are warmly British and should be the ones we use.

Andrew H.N. Gray
Edinburgh

SIR – Motoring in the southern United States, it was quite normal to turn on the radio and receive a warning that a storm was going to "barrel in". The same phrase sounds slightly ridiculous when enunciated by a newsreader with an impeccable English accent. This is becoming all too common now. Please, can a storm not simply arrive? If it could send up its card first, that would be nice.

William Smith
St Helens, Lancashire

SIR – I believe the current practice of naming storms does no good. It simply encourages them to be more violent and life-threatening. They were not named in the past and we thus had a much quieter time in the last century. We didn't have this problem when Margaret Thatcher was in charge.

David Greenway
Andover, Hampshire

SIR – Following on from the Spanish naming Storm Nelson, perhaps we could have some fun.

Storm Rishi – high winds from a southerly direction expected to blow many more migrants ashore

Storm Keir – promised a lot with consequences nationally, veered left very early on

Storm Nicola – devastated caravans and motor homes on the east coast of Scotland

Storm Humza – quickly followed Storm Nicola, blew in from the east and caused huge damage everywhere in Scotland

Storm JK – highly damaging gusts expected to lift roofs of the Scottish Parliament building

Storm Tory – an exceptionally "wet" 14-year period of damage, low-lying second homes of middle England devastated

Storm Drakeford – high winds expected but never got past 20mph in built-up areas

Storm Davey – forecast to go east, actually went west and ran out of energy very quickly

Storm Sadiq – expected to bring London to a grinding halt.

Mike Metcalfe
Butleigh, Somerset

Received punctuation

SIR – I note that current guidance from the Local Government Association states that punctuation should not be included in street signage. Residents of Westward Ho! in Devon may have cause to worry.

John Bowden
Chellaston, Derbyshire

SIR – I can understand residents' unease regarding the omission of the apostrophe in St Mary's Walk, Harrogate.

My friend was similarly unsettled when his retirement complex was named St Peter's Close.

John Catchpole
Beverley, East Yorkshire

SIR – Phase out the apostrophe in Yorkshire? Impossible. That would be t' thin end o' t' wedge.

Anthony Gibbs
Wilmslow, Cheshire

SIR – I wonder if the total number of apostrophes in daily use is actually on average remaining constant.

Those at risk of being dropped inappropriately are surely being more than compensated for by the prolific use of apostrophes in plural's such as potatoe's, bike's, taxi's and nail parlour's.

John Bath
Clevedon, North Somerset

SIR – Apostrophes are, indeed, important. That was drummed into me by various teachers during my attendance at Stationers' Company's School, in North London, from 1965–1972.

Im pleased to report thats just one of many of lifes learning's, among'st many other thing's, Ive never forgotten.

Rob Mason
Nailsea, North Somerset

SIR – Keep a lookout, at this time of year, for the ultimate apostrophe abomination, which I have only seen once, and forgot to photograph: "Xma's Tree's for sale".

Tom Hoyle
Blackburn, Lancashire

Twitter ye not

SIR – For how much longer must we see the microblogging site referred to as "X formerly Twitter"?

I thought I'd ask "*The Daily Telegraph*, formerly *The Daily Telegraph and Morning Post*, formerly *The Daily Telegraph and Courier*".

Dr Peter Swinyard
Swindon, Wiltshire

SIR – If I read the phrase "X (previously known as Twitter)" ever again I swear I will not be responsible for my actions.

Roger Andrews
Blandford, Dorset

Not safe for work

SIR – Naked Wines has warned it could go bust. Perhaps it could be rescued by a merger with Virgin Wines, creating interesting possibilities for a combined name for the new company.

Michael Hughes
Birmingham

SIR – Sir John Timpson advises that economising on office lavatory paper "makes little improvement to the bottom line". I have an uncomfortable feeling that he may be right.

David Lyall
London SW3

SIR – "Train lines get an earful over mispronouncing station names", runs your headline. Could somebody please tell me how to pronounce Yorkshire's Penistone? I'm asking on behalf of one of my now grown-up children.

Tony Parrack
London SW20

Widow's pique

SIR – The bank that owns Scottish Widows is worried that the word "widows" is "unnecessarily vivid".

More triggering than the name is the image of the widow used on the website and on advertising. With a full face of makeup and a saucy, come-hither look to camera, she is so obviously not upset by the loss of her husband that the police might want to look into his death. The marketing message seems to be, "With our payout, you can have a full makeover and get straight back in the game." Now *that's* tactful.

Cynthia Harrod-Eagles
Northwood, Middlesex

SIR – In order to avoid "triggering" anybody, perhaps Lloyds, the new owners of Scottish Widows, should just remove the vowels, as in ABRDN.

Fiona Wild
Cheltenham, Gloucestershire

SIR – Trigger warning: this book contains words, there are long words, short words and some words you will not understand. If you have any issues with this please contact our telephone hotline which will remain totally silent for fear of upsetting anyone.

Allan Evans
Mawnan Smith, Cornwall

Take a letter

SIR – If the chief investment officer Peter Branner believes media reaction to Abrdn's rebrand is "childish", perhaps he should read *Th Emprr's Nw Clths*.

Philip Davies
Newbury, Berkshire

SIR – Given the prevalence and effects of equality, diversity and inclusion (EDI) policies perhaps we should rearrange the wording to diversity, inclusion and equality (DIE). Much more appropriate.

Bob Thompson
Stoke on Trent, Staffordshire

SIR – Like many of your readers of a certain age, whose memories are not quite what they used to be, I am suffering from UAS. This has been caused by the proliferation of UA in *The Daily Telegraph* of late and I refer to Monday's article on Kate Silverton's research into ADHD which, not through ignorance, I've subsequently realised stands for Attention-Deficit/Hyperactivity Disorder. It would really help those of us suffering from UAS if you could bear this in mind in future articles [UAS – Unexplained Acronym Syndrome].

R. L. Chick
Billingshurst, West Sussex

Ending on a positive note

SIR – We are well into Lent but it's not too late for the media to resolve to abstain from using any word that ends in "ist" or "ism".

At least until Easter Sunday.

Dr P. E. Pears
Coleshill, Warwickshire

Tinker, tailor, plonker, pillock

SIR – While the BBC insists on employing Graham Norton as presenter of the Eurovision Song Contest, words such as *plonker*, *pillock* and *berk* are assured a future in common parlance.

A.M.S. Hutton-Wilson
Evercreech, Somerset

SIR – I am devastated that certain well-established words are falling out of use. I have insisted that my gravestone will bear the legend: "Here lies Anthony Bone, Cad, Bounder and Mountebank". Not strictly true (which is par for the course for most epitaphs), but it rolls off the tongue rather nicely.

Anthony Bone (not yet deceased)
Clare, Suffolk

SIR – Please be assured that terms like *pillock* and *blighter* are still very much alive, especially in many clubs, organisations and villages.

Pillock was first used in the 1500s and *Blighter* can be traced back to the 19th century. Although younger folks may not be familiar with such terms us older generations are far from familiar with terms used by the under 40s.

Is very important that such terminology lives on.

Many villages still need their pillocks and blighters.

Lyndon Yorke
Member of the Eccentric Club (number 001)
Booker Common, Buckinghamshire

DEAR
DAILY TELEGRAPH

Away from the desk

SIR – I trust that Alex is enjoying his holiday. Though I am slightly concerned for his well-being: not the fact that he has slept in a deckchair for some time, but that his wineglass appears untouched.

Richard Stewart
Bridlington, East Yorkshire

SIR – There are many headings on your front page which distress me, but the worst of them is "Matt is away".

Ron Alder
Ipswich, Suffolk

SIR – It seems that only one person understands what is going on and that is Matt. Matt for prime minister.

Sarah Crews
Plymouth, Devon

SIR – Michael Deacon for PM.

John Stevenson
Maidenhead, Berkshire

Making the headlines

SIR – In Saturday's *Daily Telegraph* an article on page 16 reported that a man had his penis cut off with a vegetable knife. On the same page almost next to this report was another article with the title of "Smaller vegetables on Tesco's shelves after floods hit farms".

You don't just throw this paper together, do you.

Richard Bowden
Droitwich, Worcestershire

SIR – I must applaud the innovative approach to Christmas catering that gave rise to your headline, "Aldi and Lidl poach millions of customers with Wagyu beef and Champagne". I would, however, think that it would be better to casserole them with a Cabernet Sauvignon and a few herbs.

Ruth Corderoy
Didcot, Oxfordshire

Food for thought

SIR – I am not sure if you know how delicious *The Daily Telegraph* is. Our cat, Dots, finds it irresistible. Your newsprint is obviously very tasty.

Barbara Jackson
Epping Upland, Essex

Photo opportunities

SIR – Apropos your picture of the Garrick Club member reading his newspaper, is this another photo-editing scandal? Where is his drink?

Mike Thompson
Paignton, Devon

SIR – In today's *Daily Telegraph*, there are pictures of Sir Keir Starmer, Angela Rayner, Jeremy Corbyn, Diane Abbott, Rishi Sunak, Ed Davey and Gary Lineker. Time to get my darts out again, I think.

Tim Rann
Mirfield, West Yorkshire

SIR – Does anybody have a photograph of Nigel Farage with his mouth closed?

Cliff Brooker
Hastings, East Sussex

Fool me once

SIR – I scoured three newspapers on Monday for the usual April Fool's Day articles and identified a number of possibilities. However, sadly I concluded that all were in fact true.

Guy Mainwaring-Burton
St John, Jersey

The solution to everything

SIR – I wonder whether the setter of the Panagram on Thursday 13 June was aware that the solution, Indemnity, was also the name of a horse running at Nottingham that afternoon, which won his race.

Please ask the Panagram setter to keep up this excellent service.

Brian Stanton
Sutton, Surrey

Have I got views for you

SIR – There was an interesting discussion on *The World at One* today regarding anger, and it was suggested that if you wrote down what had angered you on a piece of paper and then tore it up, your rage would diminish. I wondered if writing a letter full of your anger to your newspaper, which then doesn't publish it, would work the same way.

Henrietta Thewes
Edinburgh

SIR – I was at a funeral last week when an old friend I had not seen for some years came over to me and said: "I know you are not dead because I see the occasional letter from you in the *Telegraph*".

Thank you for letting my friends know I am still alive.

David Vetch
Smallfield, Surrey

SIR – For some time now, I have noticed that many of your letters page correspondents are doctors. Today's paper has six.

If they are handwritten, I wonder if you have to use the services of a retired chemist?

Dennis Rolfe
London NW3

SIR – "Your letter's been published!" I yelled with delight.

Husband's smile faded rapidly as I read it aloud. He reached for the newspaper, then said: "That's not me; we don't live in Berkshire."

Please publish the letter from the other Clive Williams. It's more interesting.

Ruth Jackson
Sidmouth, Devon

SIR – You regularly publish letters from my wife. In the interest of levelling up I ask that you publish this one.

Dr Bob Ballard
Wokingham, Berkshire

SIR – I recently bought my wife a copy of the book of unpublished letters to *The Daily Telegraph*. I'm now not sure if that was such a good idea. On the plus side I haven't been tasked with a job for absolutely ages; but the downside has been that she sits across the table from me chuckling and occasionally guffawing while I attempt the cryptic crossword.

I think that next year I shall stipulate that she reads it in another room, or better still, another house.

Mike Tugby
Warminster, Wiltshire

SIR – I wonder if it is easier to have a letter published in *The Daily Telegraph* than to have Royal Mail deliver letters on time.

Happy Christmas and New Year to all.

That's job done for this year.

Nigel Algar
Bottesford, Nottinghamshire